PROTECTION MANUAL

— FOR —

HUMAN RIGHTS DEFENDERS

RESEARCHED AND WRITTEN BY ENRIQUE EGUREN,
PEACE BRIGADES INTERNATIONAL, EUROPEAN OFFICE (PBI BEO)

PUBLISHED BY FRONT LINE
THE INTERNATIONAL FOUNDATION FOR THE PROTECTION OF
HUMAN RIGHTS DEFENDERS

I

Published by Front Line 2005
The International Foundation for the Protection of Human Rights Defenders
16 Idrone Lane, Off Bath Place, Blackrock, County Dublin, Ireland

Copies of this manual are available from
info@frontlinedefenders.org and pbibeo@biz.tiscali.be

Priced €20 plus post and packing

To request/order a Manual please contact to:

PBI-European Office
38, Rue Saint-Christophe, 1000 Bruxelles (Belgium)
Tel/fax + 32 (0)2 511 14 98
pbibeo@biz.tiscali.be

Front Line
16 Idrone lane, Off Bath Place, Blackrock, County Dublin, Ireland
tel: +353 1212 3750 fax: +353 1212 1001
protectionmanual@frontlinedefenders.org

The manual is being translated into French, Spanish, Russian and
Arabic by Front Line (as well as to several other languages)

ISBN: 0-9547883-1-1

Foreword by Hina Jilani

In my work as Special Representative of the Secretary General on Human Rights Defenders I have noted with grave concern an increase in the number of reports of serious human rights abuses against defenders and a notable shift away from low-level targeting, such as intimidation and harassment, to more serious violations, such as attacks on and threats to the physical integrity of defenders. In 2004 we worked on reports of at least 47 defenders who had been killed because of their work.

It is clear that the primary responsibility for the protection of human rights defenders lies with Governments, as set out in the UN Declaration on Human Rights Defenders[1]. We must continue to work to get all governments to take seriously their obligations in this regard and take effective measures to ensure the protection of human rights defenders.

However, the gravity of the risks faced on a daily basis by human rights defenders are such that it is also important to pursue other means to strengthen their protection. In this regard I hope that this Protection Manual will support human rights defenders in developing their own security plans and protection mechanisms. Many human rights defenders are so engaged by their work to protect others that they give insufficient attention to their own security. It is important that all of us involved in working for human rights understand that we must be concerned about security, not just for ourselves but for the people we work with and for.

Hina Jilani
UN Secretary-General's Special Representative on Human Rights Defenders

---

[1] Declaration on the Right and Responsibility of Individuals, Groups and Organs of Society to Promote and Respect Universally Recognised Human Rights and Fundamental Freedoms.

Front line

Front Line was founded in Dublin in 2001 with the specific aim of protecting Human Rights Defenders, people who work, non-violently, for any or all of the rights enshrined in the Universal Declaration of Human Rights (UDHR). Front Line aims to address some of the needs identified by defenders themselves, including protection, networking, training and access to the thematic and country mechanisms of the UN and other regional bodies.

Front Line's main focus is on those human rights defenders at risk, either temporarily or permanently because of their work on behalf of their fellow citizens. Front Line runs a small grants program to provide for the security needs of defenders. Front Line mobilizes campaigning and lobbying on behalf of defenders at immediate risk. In emergency situations Front Line can facilitate temporary relocation.

Front Line conducts research and publishes reports on the situation of human rights defenders in specific countries. The organization also develops resource materials and training packages on behalf of human rights defenders as well as facilitating networking and exchange between defenders in different parts of the world. Front Line projects are generally undertaken in partnership with specific national human rights organizations.

Front Line promotes awareness of the Universal Declaration of Human Rights and is working to ensure that the principles and standards set out in the Declaration on the Right and Responsibility of Individuals, Groups and Organs of Society to Promote and Protect Universally Recognised Human Rights and Fundamental Freedoms (known as the Declaration on Human Rights Defenders) are known, respected and adhered to worldwide.

Front Line has Special Consultative Status with the Economic and Social Council of the United Nations.

Front Line has charitable status (CHY NO 14029), is independent and impartial.

To support this work Front Line relies entirely on the generosity of individual and organizational funding. Front Line has been fortunate, since its launch in 2001, to have received funding from a variety of sources and gratefully receives donations on an individual basis.

Pbi

Peace Brigades International (PBI) is a non-governmental organization (NGO) which protects human rights defenders and promotes nonviolent transformation of conflicts.

When invited, PBI sends teams of volunteers into areas of repression and conflict. The volunteers accompany human rights defenders and their organizations when threatened by political violence. Perpetrators of human rights abuses usually do not want the world to witness their actions. The physical presence of volunteers as observers, together to their extensive networking and advocacy activities and a wide international support network help to deter hostility and attacks against defenders. In this way PBI intends to create space for human rights defenders to work for social justice and human rights. PBI has an international Board of Trustees, an International Office in London and Country or Associate Groups in 17 countries, as well as a number of Projects in the Field.

The European Office of Peace Brigades International is located in Brussels (Belgium). The contents of this Manual are one of the results of the work of its Research and Training Unit.

You can find more information on PBI at
http://www.peacebrigades.org/

and on the European Office of PBI at
http://www.peacebrigades.org/beo.html

Front Line was founded with a mandate to work exclusively for the protection of human rights defenders. Sadly our daily work brings home how much increased security and protection for human rights defenders is needed in a world where they are increasingly under attack. Our main focus is to increase pressure to hold accountable the governments who are both responsible under international human rights law for the protection of human rights defenders, and yet all too often the perpetrators of attacks and repressive measures against them. However, it is clear from the feedback of human rights defenders themselves, that much more could also be done to develop their own capacity to improve their security

We were therefore excited when we heard of the project that Peace Brigades International were developing under the title "Mainstreaming Protection, and particularly the proposed manual for human rights defenders. We swiftly agreed with them to fund the research and production of this manual.

We have been very pleased to work with Enrique Eguren as the author of the manual. Together with his colleagues he has brought a wealth of experience of security and protection issues to the task. PBI have also undertaken a number of workshops with human rights defenders in the field to try to ensure that the manual benefits from those working on the front line. Two of those workshops were undertaken in conjunction with Front Line in Bukavu and Goma, Eastern Democratic Republic of Congo in May 2004.

Front Line's objective in publishing the manual is to provide a practical resource that human rights defenders can use in developing their security and protection plans and strategies. The manual is very much offered as a work in progress upon which we hope we can build with the shared experiences of human rights defenders working in hostile environments. The contents have benefited from the discussions on security and protection at the 1st and 2nd Dublin Platforms for Human Rights Defenders held in 2002 and 2003. There will be an opportunity for structured discussion and feedback on the manual at the 3rd Dublin Platform in October 2005

The manual tries to go into some depth into how to analyze risks and threats and how to develop effective security and protection strategies and plans. It will hopefully be a useful resource for those responsible for security in human rights NGOs and as a support for training for human rights defenders. It is our intention to produce a shorter handbook of practical tips and suggestions to complement the training manual. Front Line is also engaged in a project with Privaterra to produce a manual and resource pack specifically on the issue of electronic communications and security, as partly summarized in chapter 13, which will be published in 2005.

We need to acknowledge the contribution of a number of individuals without whom this manual would not have been produced.

Marie Caraj, Pascale Boosten, Michael Schools and Christoph Klotz, dear colleagues at the European Office of PBI, were key for this project: Nothing would have been done without their commitment and experience.

The text was reviewed and edited by Mary Lawlor, Andrew Anderson, James Mehigan and Dmitri Vitaliev (Chapter 13) at Front Line. Kristin Hulaas Sunde edited an early version of the text.

Chapter 13 is based on the work of Robert Guerra, Katitza Rodríguez and Caryn Madden from Privaterra (Canada).

We are indebted to the input and comments on the draft we have received from Arnold Tsunga (Zimbabwe Lawyers for Human Rights), Sihem Bensedrine (Tunis, Conseil National pour les Libertés en Tunisie), Father Bendan Forde (Itinerant Franciscans, Colombia), Indai Sajor (former Director of the Asian Centre for Women´s Human Rights, Philippines), James Cavallaro (Brazil, Associate Director, Human Rights Program, Harvard Law School), Nadejda Marques (consultant and researcher, Global Justice Center, Rio de Janeiro, Brazil) and Marie Caraj (PBI BEO, Belgium).

Other colleagues have contributed with their own work. We have to mention José Cruz and Iduvina Hernández from SEDEM (Guatemala), Claudia Samayoa (Guatemala), Jaime Prieto (Colombia), Emma Eastwood (UK), and Cintia Lavandera at the Human Rights Defenders Program from Amnesty International in London.

Carmen Díez Rozas carefully designed the Manual and did the DTP, and Montserrat Muñoz provided advice in DTP and helped with illustrations.

We are also grateful to the support provided by Development Cooperation Ireland.

Printed by 'Print and Display'.

(From the author) Also many other people have contributed to gather the background knowledge necessary for writing the Manual. It is impossible to list all of them here, but we would like to mention a few names, such as:

To all the PBI people, and specially to my former close colleagues in the Colombia Project such as Marga, Elena, Francesc, Emma, Tomás, Juan, Mikel, Solveig, Mirjam and so many others ...

To Danilo, Clemencia and Abilio and their colleagues from the Comision Intereclesial de Justicia y Paz in Colombia. They taught to me how to live inside the heart of the people.

To the people from Santa Marta, in El Salvador, and from Cacarica, Jiguamiando and San Jose de Apartado in Colombia. They, among others, taught to me how people in the countryside live with dignity.

To the persons committed with the training program in security for defenders by the Project Counselling Service in Colombia.

To the advice and initial learning provided by REDR (London) and Koenraad van Brabant (Belgium).

And to so many defenders met in El Salvador, Guatemala, Colombia, Mexico, Sri Lanka, Croatia, Serbia, Kosovo, Rwanda, Democratic Republic of Congo, Ingushetia, etc. An ocean of conversations, tears, smiles and learning and commitment ...

Finally, nothing would have been done without the love and dedication and support from Grisela and Iker and my parents. All my love for them.

We thank all of the above, and the many human rights defenders we have worked with and learned from, for their input. However, the final text, and any errors which may be contained in it, are the joint responsibility of Front Line and PBI. We hope that this manual will be a useful tool in improving the protection and security of human rights defenders, although we know that it provides no guarantees, and that in the end these are issues which each person must take responsibility for themselves. We look forward to your feedback.

Front Line
Peace Brigades International
March 7th, 2005

Disclaimer

The contents of this manual do not necessarily represent the positions of Peace Brigades International Front Line (International Foundation for the Protection of Human Rights Defenders).

Neither the authors nor the publisher warrant that the information contained in this publication is complete and correct and shall not be liable for any damages incurred as a result of its use. No part of this manual can be taken as a norm or taken as a guarantee or used without the necessary criteria to assess the risk and security problems a defender may face.

Index of Chapters

A security and protection manual for human rights defenders

Human rights defenders at risk

Human Rights are guaranteed under international law but working to ensure that they are realised and taking up the cases of those who have had their rights violated can be a dangerous business in countries all around the world. Human Rights Defenders are often the only force standing between ordinary people and the unbridled power of the state. They are vital to the development of democratic processes and institutions, ending impunity and the promotion and protection of human rights.

Human Rights Defenders often face harassment, detention, torture, defamation, suspension from their employment, denial of freedom of movement and difficulty in obtaining legal recognition for their associations. In some countries they are killed or "disappeared."

Over the last few years, general awareness has increased of the enormous risk human rights defenders face in their work. The risk is easy to identify when defenders work in hostile situations, for instance, if a country's laws penalise people who do certain types of human rights work. Defenders are also at risk when the law fully sanctions human rights work on the one hand, but fails to punish those who threaten or attack defenders on the other. In armed conflict situations, the risk becomes even higher.

Apart from a few chaotic situations during which a defender's life may be in the hands of soldiers at a checkpoint, the violence committed against defenders can't be called indiscriminate. In most cases, violent attacks are a deliberate and well-planned response to defenders' work, and linked to a clear political or military agenda.

These challenges require human rights defenders to implement comprehensive and dynamic security strategies in their day to day work. Giving defenders well-meant advice or recommending that they "take care" is not enough. Better security management is key. This manual does not offer tailor-made solutions ready to be applied to any scenario. However, it does try to provide a set of strategies aimed at improving defenders' security management.

The most effective security lessons come from defenders themselves - from their daily experiences and the tactics and strategies they develop over time in order to protect others and their own working environments. This manual must therefore be understood as a work in progress which will need to be updated and adapted as we gather more input from human rights defenders working on the front line.

There are also lessons to be learned from international humanitarian NGOs, who have recently started to develop their own rules and procedures to maintain staff security.

It is important to be aware that the main risk for defenders is that threats often materialise into actual attacks. Aggressors have the will, the means and the impunity to put threats into action. The best tool for protecting defenders is therefore political action to address the one, big, remaining issue: The need for governments and civil society to put pressure on and act against those who day after day threaten, harass and kill defenders. The advice given in this manual is in no way intended to replace the due responsibility of each and all governments to protect human rights defenders.

That said, defenders can significantly improve their security by following a few tried and tested rules and procedures.

This manual is a humble contribution to an aim shared by many different organisations: To preserve the invaluable work that human rights defenders do. They are the ones on the front line, and they are also the main characters of this manual.

The manual

The purpose of this manual is to provide human rights defenders with additional knowledge and some tools that may be useful for improving their understanding of security and protection. It is hoped that the manual will support training on security and protection and will help defenders to undertake their own risk assessments and define security rules and procedures which suit their particular situation.

This manual is the result of a long term project by PBI on field protection for defenders. We have had the opportunity to learn from and share experiences and knowledge with hundreds of defenders in the field, as well as in workshops, meetings and discussions about security. Most of the manual's contents have already been applied in practice, either in protection work or in training workshops with defenders. This manual is the fruit of all these exchanges, and we owe the defenders involved a huge thanks for their input.

Security and protection are difficult areas. They are based around structured knowledge, but also influenced by individual attitudes and organisational behaviour. One of the key messages in this manual is to give the issue of security the time, space and energy it deserves, despite overloaded work agendas and the severe stress and fear all defenders and their organisations are under. This means going beyond people's individual knowledge about security and moving towards an organisational culture in which security is inherent.

Knowing enough about a conflict scenario and understanding the local political logic are also key to proper management of defenders' security. This manual contains an overall framework as well as a step by step approach for managing security. It also includes some reflections on basic concepts like risk, vulnerability and threat, and a few suggestions for how to improve and develop security for defenders in their day to day work. We hope that the topics covered will allow NGOs and defenders to plan for and cope with the increasing security challenges involved in human rights work.

This said, the first thing we wish to remind all of us is that defenders risk their well-being and their lives, and this is serious stuff. Sometimes the only way to save a life is just going into hiding and then fleeing. We want to leave it very clear that all the techniques and suggestions in this manual are not, by any means, the only way to think about security issues for defenders. The manual has been written in good faith but sadly offers no guarantee of success.

Let's improve this Manual...

The manual is a work in progress, and will need to be developed, improved and refined over time. Your feedback as a defender on any aspect of this manual will be invaluable:

Please send any comments and opinions - particularly in terms of your experiences of using the manual in your work. With your help, we can make this manual an increasingly useful tool for defenders all over the world.

Email to any of us:

- protectionmanual@frontlinedefenders.org

- pbibeo@biz.tiscali.be

Or by post to Front Line or PBI

□ PBI- European Office
38, Rue Saint-Christophe, 1000 Bruxelles (Belgium)
Tel/fax + 32 (0)2 511 14 98

□ Front Line
16 Idrone lane, Off Bath Place, Blackrock, County Dublin, Ireland
tel: +353 1212 3750 fax: +353 1212 1001

A short introduction to Human Rights Defenders

"Human rights defender" is a term used to describe people who, individually or with others, take action to promote or protect human rights. Human rights defenders are identified above all by what they do, and the term can therefore best be explained by describing their actions and some of the contexts they work in.

In 1998 the United National General Assembly approved the "Declaration on the Right and Responsibility of Individuals, Groups and Organs of Society to Promote and Protect Universally Recognized Human Rights and Fundamental Freedoms" (Hereafter the "UN Declaration on Human Rights Defenders"). In other words, fifty years after the Universal Declaration of Human Rights, and after twenty years of negotiations on a draft declaration on human rights defenders, the United Nations finally recognized what is a reality: that thousands of people were promoting and contributing to the protection of human rights throughout the world. This is an inclusive Declaration that honours the amount and variety of people engaged in the promotion and protection of human rights.

The Special Representative of the UN Secretary General on Human Rights Defenders is mandated "to seek, receive examine and respond to information on the situation and the rights of anyone, acting individually or in association with others, to promote and protect human rights and fundamental freedoms."

Front Line defines a human rights defender as "a person who works, non-violen-tly, for any or all of the rights enshrined in the Universal Declaration of Human Rights." Front Line seeks to promote the UN Declaration on Human Rights Defenders (see page 113 for the full text of the Declaration).

Who is responsible for protecting human rights defenders?

The Declaration on Human Rights Defenders stresses that the state is primarily responsible for protecting human rights defenders. It also acknowledges *"the valuable work of individuals, groups and associations in contributing to the effective elimination of all violations of human rights and fundamental freedoms"* and *"the relationship between international peace and security and the enjoyment of human rights and fundamental freedoms"*.

But according to Hina Jilani, Special Representative of the UN General Secretary on Human Rights Defenders, *"exposing human rights violations and seeking redress for them is largely dependent on the degree of security enjoyed by human rights defenders"*[1]. A look at any report on human rights defenders throughout the world reveals stories of torture, disappearances, killings, threats, robbery, break-ins to offices, harassment, illegal detentions, being subjected to intelligence and surveillance activities, etc. Unfortunately, this is the rule and not the exception for defenders.

---

[1] Report on Human Rights Defenders, 10 Sept 2001 (A/56/341).

Suggested further reading

To find out more about human rights defenders, visit:

☐ www.unhchr.ch/defender/about1.htm (The UN High Commissioner on Human Rights).

☐ www.frontlinedefenders.org (Front Line, The International Foundation for Human Rights Defenders).

☐ www.peacebrigades.org/beo.html (The European Office of Peace Brigades International in Brussels).

☐ The Observatory for the Protection of Human Rights Defenders, created by the International Federation on Human Rights (FIDH; www.fidh.org) and the World Organisation Against Torture
(OMCT; www.omct.org).

☐ Amnesty International: www.amnesty.org and
http://web.amnesty.org/pages/hrd-index-eng

☐ www.ishr.ch, see under "HRDO" (The HRD Office of the International Service for Human Rights in Geneva).

☐ www.humanrightsfirst.org (Human Rights First).

☐ www.urgentactionfund.org (Urgent Action Fund for Women's Human Rights).

To learn more about existing international legal instruments and the UN Declaration on Human Rights Defenders, visit :

☐ www.unhchr.ch : This is the web site of the UN High Commissioner for Human Rights.

☐ www.frontlinedefenders.org/manual/en/index.htm (Front Line, Ireland), for a manual on international instruments for human rights defenders. Their links page is very useful also:
http://www.frontlinedefenders.org/links/

☐ www.ishr.ch/index.htm (International Service for Human Rights, Geneva), for a compilation of international and regional instruments for the protection of human rights defenders.

CHAPTER 1

Making informed decisions about security and protection

Purpose

To become aware of the importance of analysing your working environment for security reasons.

To learn different methods for undertaking context and stakeholder analyses.

Human rights defenders' working environments

Human rights defenders usually work in complex environments, where there are many different actors, and which are influenced by deeply political decision-making processes. Many things will be happening almost simultaneously, with each event impacting on another. The dynamics of each actor, or stakeholder, in this scenario will play a significant role in that actor's relationships with others. Human rights defenders therefore need information not only about issues directly related to their work, but also about the positions of key actors and stakeholders.

A simple exercise would be to organize a group brainstorming to try to identify and list all the social, political and economic actors that may have an influence on your current security situation.

Analysing your working environment

It is very important to know and understand as much as possible about the context you are working in. A good analysis of that context enables informed decisions about which security rules and procedures to apply. It is also important to think about possible future scenarios, in order, where possible, to take preventive action.

However, simply analysing your working environment isn't enough. You also need to look at how each intervention could affect the situation and how other actors might react to each one. It is also important to take into account the dimensions of a work scenario. You can undertake an analysis at **macro** level by studying a country or a region, but you also have to find out how those macro dynamics function in the particular area where you are working, i.e. the **micro** dynamics. For instance, paramilitaries in one local area may act differently to how you might expect following a regional or national analysis. You need to be aware of such local characteristics. It is also crucial to avoid having a fixed view of a work scenario, because situations evolve and change. They should therefore be reviewed regularly.

Asking Questions, the ***Force Field Analysis*** and the ***Stakeholder Analysis*** are three useful methods for analysing your working environment:

Asking questions

You can understand your working environment better simply by asking the right questions about it. This is a useful tool for generating discussions in a small group, but it will only work if the questions are formulated in a way that will make it easy to find a solution.

Suppose, for example, that harassment by local authorities has become a problem. If you phrase the question as: "What should be done to reduce the harassment?", you may find yourselves simply looking for a remedy to a symptom, i.e. the harassment.

But if you phrase the question to point toward a solution, you may be on your way to finding a real solution. For example, if you ask: "Is our socio-political environment safe enough for doing our work?", there can be only two answers – yes or no.

If the answer is yes, you will need to formulate another question that can help you pin-point and properly understand the critical issues at stake for maintaining your safety. If, after proper consideration of all available activities, plans and resources, as well as legislation, negotiations, comparisons with other defenders in the area, etc, the answer should turn out to be no, this in itself will amount to a solution to your security problem.

Using the Asking Questions method:

> ◆ Look for questions that will help you pin-point and properly understand the critical issues at stake for maintaining your safety.
> ◆ Formulate the questions in a solution-oriented way.
> ◆ Repeat this process as many times as necessary (as a discussion).

Some useful questions to be asked:

> ◆ Which are the key issues at stake in the socio-political and economy arena?
> ◆ Who are the key stakeholders in relation to these key issues?
> ◆ How might our work affect negatively or positively the interests of these key stakeholders?
> ◆ How might we react if we became targeted by any of these actors due to our work?
> ◆ Is our socio-political environment safe enough for doing our work?

* How have local/national authorities responded to previous work of rights defenders related to this issue?

* How have the key stakeholders responded to previous or similar work of rights defenders or others related to these issues?

* How have the media and the community responded in similar circumstances?

* Etc.

Force Field Analysis

Force field analysis is a technique which can help you visually identify how different forces are helping or hindering the achievement of your work objectives. It shows both supporting and resisting forces, and works on the assumption that security problems might arise from resisting forces, and that you could take advantage of some of the supporting forces. This technique can be completed by just one person, but is most effective when used by a diverse group with a clearly defined work objective and a method for accomplishing it.

Begin by drawing a horizontal arrow pointing to a box. Write a short summary of your work objective in this box. This will provide a focus for identifying supporting and resisting forces. Draw another box above the central arrow. List all potential forces which could be preventing you from achieving your work objective here. Draw a similar box, containing all potential supportive forces, underneath the arrow. Draw a final box for forces whose direction is unknown or unsure.

Chart 1: Force field analysis for assessing working environment

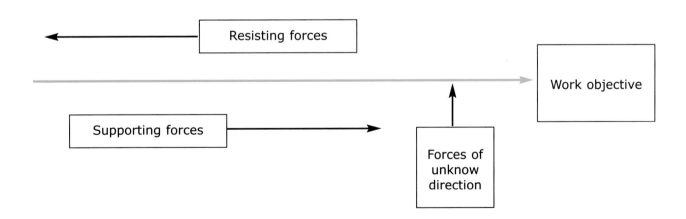

After completing your chart it is time to evaluate the results. Force field analysis helps you to clearly visualise the forces you are dealing with. The goal is to find ways to reduce or eliminate risk generated by resisting forces, partly through potential help from supporting forces. In terms of the forces of unknown direction, you will need to decide whether to look at them as supporting, or to monitor them continuously in order to detect signs of them becoming either resisting or supporting.

For example:

Imagine that you belong to an organisation dealing with indigenous people's rights to natural resources on their own land. There are ongoing conflicts between a number of stakeholders about the exploitation of those resources. You now want to extend your work to a neighbouring area with similar problems.

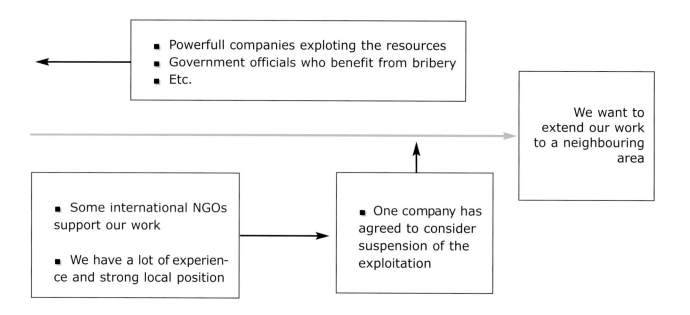

Actors (or stakeholders) Analysis

Actors or stakeholder analysis is an important way of increasing the information you have available when making decisions about protection. It involves identifying and describing the different actors or stakeholders involved and their relationships, on the basis of their characteristics and interests – all in relation to a given protection issue.

> **A stakeholder in protection is any person, group or institution with an interest in, or involvement in, a policy outcome in the area of protection[1].**

A stakeholder analysis is key to understanding:

- Who is a stakeholder and under what circumstances their "stake" counts.
- The relationships between stakeholders in protection, their characteristics and interests.
- How these will be affected by protection activities.
- Each stakeholder's willingness to become involved in those protection activities.

---

[1] Adapted from *Sustainable Livelihoods Guidance Sheets* No. 5.4 (2000)

Stakeholders in protection can be categorised in the following way:

Primary stakeholders. In a protection context, these are **the defenders themselves, and those they work with and for**, because they all have a primary stake in their own protection.

Duty-bearer stakeholders, who are responsible for protecting defenders, i.e.:

⬧ Government and state institutions (including security forces, judges, legislators, etc.)

⬧ International bodies with a mandate that includes protection, such as some UN bodies, regional IGOs, peacekeeping forces, etc.

⬧ In the case of opposition armed actors, they can be held accountable for not attacking the defenders (as the civilian population they are), specially when these actors control the territory.

Key stakeholders, **who can significantly influence the protection of defenders.** They may have political clout or the capacity to put pressure on duty-bearer stakeholders who do not fulfil their responsibilities (such s other governments, UN bodies, ICRC, etc), and similarly some of them may be often directly or indirectly involved in attacks and pressure against defenders (such as private corporations or the mass media or other governments also). All depends on the context and interests and strategies of each of these key stakeholders. A non-exhaustive list could include:

⬧ UN bodies (other than mandated ones).

⬧ The International Committee of the Red Cross (ICRC).

⬧ Other governments and multilateral institutions (both as donors and policy-makers).

⬧ Other armed actors.

⬧ NGOs (either national or international).

⬧ Churches and religious institutions.

⬧ Private corporations.

⬧ The mass media.

A major difficulty with establishing which strategies and actions are being under-taken by stakeholders is that the relationships between them are not clear-cut, or may even be non-existent. Many duty-bearer stakeholders, particularly governments, security forces and opposition armed forces, cause or contribute to human rights violations and a lack of protection for defenders. Some stakeholders, who would otherwise share the same protection concerns, may also have competing interests, such as among other governments, UN bodies and NGOs. These factors, along with those inherent in conflict scenarios, project a complex picture of the working environment as a whole.

ANALYSING CHANGING STRUCTURES AND PROCESSES

Stakeholders are not static actors. They relate to each other at multiple levels, creating a dense web of relationships. In terms of protection, it is important to highlight and pay attention to relationships which shape and transform people's protection needs. We can talk about **structures and processes**.

Structures are interrelated parts of the public sector, civil society or private bodies. We will look at them from the point of view of protection. Within the public sector, we could look at a government as a set of actors with either one unified strategy or with confronting internal strategies. For example, we could find strong discrepancies between the Ministry of Defence and the Ministry of Foreign Affairs when discussing policies related to human rights defenders, or between the Ombudsman's office and the military. Structures can have mixed components; for example, an inter-sectoral commission (members from the government, NGOs, the UN and diplomatic corps) could be created to follow up on the protection situation of a given human rights defenders organisation.

Processes are the chains of decisions and actions taken by one or more structures with the goal of improving the protection situation of a given group. There can be legislative processes, cultural processes and policy processes. Not all processes are successful in achieving improvements in protection: On many occasions protection processes are in conflict or render each other ineffective. For example, people allegedly being protected may not accept a policy protection process led by the government, because they see it as having an implicit aim of displacing people from an area. The UN and NGOs may support people in this process.

There are a number of ways to do a stakeholder analysis. The following uses a straight-forward methodology, which is key to getting good results in analyses and decision making processes.

When assessing protection processes it is important to look at them with an adequate time perspective and always take into account the interests and objectives of all stakeholders involved.

A stakeholder analysis in four steps:

1 ◆ Identify the wider protection issue (i.e. the security situation of human rights defenders in a given region within a country).

2 ◆ Who are the stakeholders? (Namely, which are the institutions and groups and individuals with a responsibility or an interest in protection?) Identify and list all stakeholders relevant to that protection issue, through brainstorms and discussions.

3 ◆ Investigate and analyse the stakeholders' characteristics and particular attributes, such as responsibilities in protection, the power to influence the protection situation, aims, strategies, legitimacy and interests (including the will to contribute to protection).

4 ◆ Investigate and analyse relationships between stakeholders.

After undertaking this analysis, you may wish to use a matrix like the following.

Place the list with all stakeholders relevant to a well-defined protection issue in a matrix (see Chart 2): Repeat the same list in the first column and along the first row. After this, you can undertake two kind of analysis:

☐ To analyse the attributes of each stakeholder (aims and interests, strategies, legitimacy and power), fill in the boxes in the diagonal line where each stakeholder intersects with itself:

For example:

You can place the aims and interests and strategies of armed opposition groups in the box "A".

☐ To analyse the relationships between stakeholders, fill in those boxes that define the most important relationships in relation to the protection issue, for example, the one which intersects between the army and the United Nations High Commissioner for Refugees (UNHCR), in box "B", and so on.

After filling the most relevant boxes, you will have a picture of the aims and strategies and interaction among main stakeholders in relation to a given protection issue.

Chart 2: A matrix system for stakeholder analysis

	GOVERN-MENT	ARMY	POLICE	ARMED OPPOSI-TION GROUP	NATIONAL HUMAN RIGHTS NGOs	CHURCHES	OTHER GOVERN-MENTS	UN AGENCIES	INTER-NATIO NAL NGO
GOVERNMENT	(stake-holder)								
ARMY		(stake-holder)						**B**	
POLICE			(stake-holder)						
ARMED OPPOSITION GROUPS				**A**					
NATIONAL HUMAN RIGHTS NGOs					(stake-holder)				
CHURCHES						(stake-holder)			
OTHER GOVERNMENTS							(stake-holder)		
UN AGENCIES								(stake-holder)	
INTERNATIONAL NGOs									(stake-holder)

Box "**A**"

FOR EACH STAKEHOLDER:

- aims and interests
- strategies
- legitimacy
- power

Box "**B**"

INTERRELATIONSHIP BETWEEN STAKEHOLDERS:

(interrelationship in relation to the protection issue and in relation to strategic issues for both stakeholders)

Assessing risk: threats, vunerabilities and capacities

Purpose

Understanding the concepts of threats, vulnerability and capacity in security.

Learning how to do a risk assessment.

Risk analysis and protection needs

Human rights defenders' work can have a negative impact on specific actors' interests, and this can in turn put defenders at risk. It is therefore important to stress that **risk is an inherent part of defenders' lives in certain countries**.

The issue of risk can be broken down in the following way:

> Analyse main stakeholders' interests and strategies ⇨ Assess impact of defenders' work on those interests and strategies ⇨ Assess threat against defenders ⇨ Assess vulnerabilities and capacities of defenders ⇨ Establish Risk.

In other words, the work you do as a defender may increase the risk you face.

☐ **What** you do can lead to threats.

☐ **How**, **where**, and **when** you work raises issues about your vulnerabilities and capacities.

There is no widely accepted definition of risk, but we can say that risk refers to possible events, however uncertain, that result in harm.

In any given situation, everyone working on human rights may face a common level of danger, but not everyone is equally vulnerable to that general **risk** just by being in the same place. **Vulnerability** - the possibility that a defender or a group will suffer an attack or harm - varies according to several factors, as we will see now.

An example:

There may be a country where the Government poses a general threat against all kinds of human rights work. This means that all defenders could be at risk. But we also know that some defenders are more at risk than others; for instance, a large, well established NGO based in the capital will probably not be as vulnerable as a small, local NGO. We might say that this is common sense, but it can be interesting to analyse why this happens in order to better understand and address the security problems of defenders.

The level of risk facing a group of defenders increases in accordance with **threats** that have been received and their **vulnerability** to those threats, as presented in this equation[1]:

$$\textbf{RISK} \quad = \quad \textbf{THREATS} \quad \textbf{X} \quad \textbf{VULNERABILITIES}$$

Threats represent the possibility that someone will harm somebody else's physical or moral integrity or property through purposeful and often violent action[2]. Making a threat assessment means analysing the likelihood of a threat being put into action.

Defenders can face many different threats in a conflict scenario, including targeting, common crime and indirect threats.

The most common type of threat – **targeting** – aims to hinder or change a group's work, or to influence the behaviour of the people involved. Targeting is usually closely related to the work done by the defenders in question, as well as to the interests and needs of the people who are opposed to the defenders' work.

Defenders may face the threat of **common criminal attacks**, especially if their work brings them to risky areas. Many cases of targeting are carried out under the guise of being 'ordinary' criminal incidents.

Indirect threats arise from the potential harm caused by fighting in armed conflicts, such as 'being in the wrong place at the wrong time'. This applies specially to defenders working in areas with armed conflict.

Targeting (targeted threats) can also be seen in a complementary way: Human rights defenders may come across **declared** threats, for example by receiving

> A summary of kinds of threats
>
> ◾ Targeting (declared threats, possible threats): threats due to your work.
>
> ◾ Threats by common criminal attacks.
>
> ◾ Indirect threats: Threats due to fighting in armed conflicts.

---

[1] Van Brabant (2000) and REDR.
[2] Dworken (1999).

a death threat (see Chapter 3, for how to assess declared threats). There are also cases of **possible** threats, when a defender close to your work is threatened and there are reasons to believe that you might be threatened next.

Vulnerabilities

Vulnerability means the degree to which people are susceptible to loss, damage, suffering and death in the event of an attack. This varies for each defender or group, and changes with time. Vulnerability is always relative, because all people and groups are vulnerable to some extent. However, everyone has their own level and type of vulnerability, depending on their circumstances. Let's see some examples:

☐ Vulnerability can be about location. For example, a defender is usually more vulnerable when s/he is out on the road during a field visit than when s/he is at a well known office where any attack is likely to be witnessed.

☐ Vulnerabilities can include lack of access to a phone or to safe ground transportation or to proper locks in the doors of a house. But vulnerabilities are also related to the lack of networks and shared responses among defenders.

☐ Vulnerabilities may also have to do with team work and fear: A defender that receives a threat may feel fear, and his/her work will be affected by fear. If s/he has no a proper way to deal with fear (somebody to talk to, a good team of colleagues, etc) chances are that s/he could makes mistakes or take poor decisions that may lead him/her to more security problems.

(There is a combined check-list of possible vulnerabilities and capacities at the end of this chapter).

Capacities

Capacities are the strengths and resources a group or defender can access to achieve a reasonable degree of security. Examples of capacities could be training in security or legal issues, a group working together as a team, access to a phone and safe transportation, to good networks of defenders, to a proper way of dealing with fear, etc.

In most cases, vulnerabilities and capacities are two sides of the same coin.

For example:

Not knowing enough about your work environment work is a vulnerability, while having this knowledge is a capacity. The same can be said about having or not access to safe transportation or to good networks of defenders.

(There is a combined check-list of possible vulnerabilities and capacities at the end of this chapter).

The risk created by threats and vulnerabilities can be reduced if defenders have enough capacities (the more capacities, the lesser the risk).

$$\text{Risk} = \frac{\text{threats} \ \times \ \text{vulnerability}}{\text{capacities}}$$

In summary,

in order to reduce risk to acceptable levels -namely, to protect- you must:

- Reduce threats.
- Reduce vulnerability factors.
- Increase protection capacities.

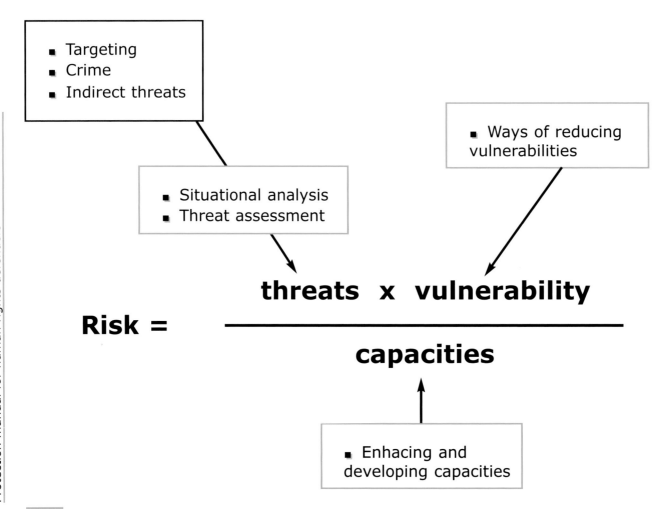

Risk is a dynamic concept that changes with time and with variations in the nature of threats, vulnerabilities and capacities. This means risk must be assessed periodically, especially if your working environment, threats or vulnerabilities change. For instance, Vulnerabilities can also increase if a change of leadership leaves a group of defenders in a weaker position than before. Risk increases dramatically with a clear and present threat. In such cases, it is not safe to try to reduce risk by increasing capacities, because that takes time.

Security measures, such as legal training or protective barriers, could reduce risk by reducing vulnerability factors. However, such measures do not confront the main source of risk, i.e. the threats, nor the will to carry them out, especially in situations where perpetrators know they are likely to go unpunished. All major interventions in protection should therefore aim to reduce threats, in addition to reducing vulnerability and enhancing capacity.

An example:

A small group of defenders are working on land property issues in a town. When their work starts affecting the local landowner's interests they receive a clear death threat. If you apply the risk equation to their security situation, you'll see that the risk these defenders face is very high, above all due to the death threat. If you want to reduce that risk it is probably not the moment to start changing the locks on the door of their office (because the risk is not related to a break-in at the office), nor the moment to buy a cell phone for each defender (even if communication might be important to security it is unlikely to be enough if there is someone coming to kill you). In this case, a more relevant strategy would be to work on networking and generating political responses to directly confront the threat (and if that is unlikely to be effective quickly the only way to reduce the risk significantly might be to reduce the defenders exposure, perhaps by moving away for a while – being able to relocate to a safe place is also a capacity).

Vulnerabilities and capacities, as well as some threats, may vary according to gender and age. You therefore need to break down your findings accordingly.

Vulnerabilities and capacities assessment

Designing a vulnerability and capacities assessment for a given group (or person) involves defining the group itself (a community, collective, NGO, individuals, etc), the physical area where it is located and the time line (your vulnerability profile will change and evolve over time). Then you can proceed to assess vulnerabilities and capacities, using the **chart 3** at the end of this chapter as a guidance.

Please note: The vulnerabilities and capacities assessment must be seen as an open-ended activity aimed at building on existing information to maintain an accurate picture of a constantly evolving situation. When assessing capacities, it is important to establish what the actual current capacities are instead of listing potential, desirable ones.

Coping and response strategies

Defenders and groups under threat use different **coping strategies** to deal with the risks they perceive that they face. These strategies will vary a lot depending on their environment (rural, urban), the type of threat, the social, financial and legal resources available, etc.

Most coping strategies can be implemented immediately and in response to short term objectives. They will therefore function more like tactics than as detailed response strategies. Most strategies also respond to individual people's subjective perceptions of risk, and could at times cause the group some level of harm, especially if the strategies used cannot be reversed.

Coping strategies are closely related to the type and severity of threat and to the group's capacities and vulnerabilities.

When thinking about security and protection you must take into account both your own and other people's coping strategies. Reinforce the effective ones, try to limit harmful ones and try to respect the remaining ones (especially coping strategies linked to cultural or religious beliefs).

Some coping strategies:

□ Reinforcing protective barriers, hiding valuables.

□ Avoiding behaviour which could be questioned by another actor, especially if control of the territory where you are working is under military dispute.

□ Going into hiding during high risk situations, including in places that are difficult to access, like mountains or jungle, changing houses, etc. Sometimes whole families go into hiding, and sometimes just defenders. Hiding could take place at night or go on for several weeks, and might involve no outside contact.

□ Looking for armed or political protection from one of the armed actors.

□ Suspending activities, closing down the office, evacuating. Forced migration (internal displacement or as refugees) or going into exile.

□ Relying on "good luck" or resorting to "magic" beliefs.

□ Becoming more secretive, including with colleagues; going into denial by refusing to discuss threats; excessive drinking, overwork, erratic behaviour.

Defenders also have access to response strategies. These can include issuing reports to publicise a specific issue, making allegations, staging demonstrations, etc. In many cases these strategies do not amount to a long term strategy, but respond to short term needs. In some cases the response strategies might even create more security problems than those they were intended to address.

When analysing coping and response strategies, take the following into account:

❑ Sensitivity: Can your strategies respond quickly to individual or group security needs?

❑ Adaptability: Can your strategies be quickly adapted to new circumstances, once the risk of attack is over? A defender may have several options available, for example to either hide or to live at other people's houses for a while. Such strategies may seem weak or unstable, but often have great endurance.

❑ Sustainability: Can your strategies endure over time, despite threats or non-lethal attacks?

❑ Effectiveness: Can your strategies adequately protect the people or groups in question?

❑ Reversibility: If your strategies don't work or the situation changes, can your strategies be reversed or changed?

Dealing with risk after doing a risk assessment

Once your risk assessment has been done, you need to look at the results. As it is impossible to measure the "amount" of risk you are facing, you need to establish an understanding of what the **level** of risk is.

Different defenders and organisations may estimate different levels of risk. What is unacceptable for some defenders can be acceptable for others, and the same can be said for people within the same organisation. Rather than discussing what "must" be done or whether you are prepared for going ahead with it, people's different thresholds of risk must be addressed: You must find a commonly acceptable threshold for all members of the group.

That said, there are different ways of dealing with risk:

◆ You can **accept** the risk as it stands, because you feel able to live with it.

◆ You can **reduce** the risk, by working on threats, vulnerabilities and capacities.

◆ You can **share** the risk, by undertaking joint actions with other defenders to make potential threats to one defender or organisation less effective.

◆ You can choose to **avoid** the risk, by changing or stopping your activities or changing approach to reduce potential threats.

◆ You can **ignore** the risk, by looking the other way. Needless to say, this is not the best option.

Bear in mind that the levels of risk are usually different for each of the organizations and individuals involved in a human rights case, and that attackers usually tend to hit in the weakest parts, so that you have to pay attention to these different levels of risk and take specific measures. For example, let's look at a case of a peasant killed by a landowner private army. There may be several organizations and individuals involved in it, such as a group of lawyers from the close-by capital city, a local peasant union and three witnesses (peasants who live in a nearby village). It is key to assess the different levels of risk of each of these stakeholders in order to plan properly for the security of each of them.

Chart 3: Information needed to assess a group's vulnerabilities and capacities

(Note: Generally speaking, the information from the column to the right may show that a given component -on the column to the left- is either a vulnerability or a capacity of a given defender or group of defenders).

COMPONENTS OF VULNERABILITIES AND CAPACITIES	INFORMATION NEEDED TO ASSESS THE VULNERABILITIES OR CAPACITIES OF THOSE COMPONENTS
GEOGRAPHICAL, PHYSICAL AND TECHNICAL COMPONENTS	
EXPOSURE	The need to be in, or to pass through, dangerous areas to carry out normal daily or occasional activities. Threatening actors in those areas.
PHYSICAL STRUCTURES	The characteristics of housing (offices, homes, shelters); building materials, doors, windows, cupboards. Protective barriers. Night lights.
OFFICES AND PLACES OPEN TO PUBLIC	Are your offices open to visitors from the general public? Are there areas reserved only for personnel? Do you have to deal with unknown people that come to your place?
HIDING PLACES, ESCAPE ROUTES	Are there any hiding places? How accessible are they (physical distance) and to whom (for specific individuals or the whole group)? Can you leave the area for a while if necessary?
ACCESS TO THE AREA	How difficult is it for outside visitors (government officials, NGOs, etc.) to access the area, for example in a dangerous neighbourhood? How difficult is access for threatening actors?
TRANSPORT AND ACCOMMODATION	Do defenders have access to safe transportation (public or private)? Do these have particular advantages or disadvantages? Do defenders have access to safe accommodation when travelling?
COMMUNICATION	Are telecommunications systems in place (radio, telephone)? Do defenders have easy access to them? Do they work properly at all times? Can they be cut by threatening actors before an attack?

COMPONENTS OF VULNERABILITIES AND CAPACITIES	INFORMATION NEEDED TO ASSESS THE VULNERABILITIES OR CAPACITIES OF THOSE COMPONENTS
COMPONENTS LINKED TO CONFLICT	
LINKS TO CONFLICT PARTIES	Do defenders have links with conflict parties (relatives, from the same area, same interests) that could be unfairly used against the defenders?
DEFENDERS' ACTIVITIES AFFECTING A CONFLICT PARTY	Do defenders' work directly affect an actor´s interests? (For example, when protecting valuable natural resources, the right to land, or similar potential targets for powerful actors) Do you work on a specially sensitive issue for powerful actors (such as land ownership, for example)?
TRANSPORTATION OF ITEMS AND GOODS AND WRITTEN INFORMATION	Do defenders have items or goods that could be valuable to armed groups, and therefore increase the risk of targeting (petrol, humanitarian aid, batteries, human rigths manuals, health manuals, etc.)?
KNOWLEDGE ABOUT FIGHTING AND MINED AREAS	Do you have information about the fighting areas that could put you at a risk? And about safe areas to help your security? Do you have reliable information about mined areas?
COMPONENTS LINKED TO THE LEGAL AND POLITICAL SYSTEM	
ACCESS TO AUTHORITIES AND TO A LEGAL SYSTEM TO CLAIM YOUR RIGHTS	Can defenders start legal processes to claim their rights? (Access to legal representation, physical presence at trials or meetings, etc.) Can defenders gain appropiate assistance from relevant authorities towards their work and protection needs?
ABILITY TO GET RESULTS FROM THE LEGAL SYSTEM AND FROM AUTHORITIES	Are defenders legally entitled to claim their rights? Or are they subjects to repressive internal laws? Can they gain enough clout to make authorities take note of their claims?
REGISTRATION, CAPACITY TO KEEP ACCOUNTS AND LEGAL STANDARS	Are defenders denied legal registration or subjected to long delays? Is their organisation able to keep proper accounts and meet national legal standards? Do you use pirate computer software?
MANAGEMENT OF INFORMATION	
SOURCES AND ACCURACY OF INFORMATION	Do defenders have reliable sources of information to base accusations on? Do defenders publicise information with the necessary accuracy and method?
KEEPING, SENDING AND RECEIVING INFORMATION	Can defenders keep information in a safe and reliable place? Could it get stolen? Can it be protected from viruses and hackers? Can you send and receive information safely?
BEING WITNESSES OR HAVING KEY INFORMATION	Are defenders key witnesses to raise charges against a powerful actor? Do defenders have relevant and unique information for a given case or process?
HAVING COHERENT AND ACCEPTABLE EXPLANATION ABOUT YOUR WORK AND AIMS	Do the defenders have a clear, sustainable and coherent explanation of their work and objectives? Is this explanation acceptable, or at least tolerated, by most/all stakeholders (specially armed ones)? Are all members of the group able to provide this explanation when requested?

Components of vulnerabilities and capacities	Information needed to assess the vulnerabilities or capacities of those components
Social and organisational components	
Existence of a group structure	Is the group structured or organised in any way? Does this structure provide an acceptable level of cohesiveness to the group?
Ability to make joint decisions	Does the group´s structure reflect particular interests or represent the whole group (extent of membership)? Are the main responsibilities carried out and decision-making done by only one or a few people? Are back-up systems in place for decision-making and responsibilities? To what degree is decision-making participatory? Does the group´s structure allow for: a) joint decision making and implementation, b) discussing issues together, c) sporadic, ineffective meetings, d) none of the above?
Security plans and procedures	Are security rules and procedures in place? Is there a broad understanding and ownership of security procedures? Do people follow the security rules? (For more details, please see Chapter 8)
Security management outside of work (family and free time)	How do defenders manage their time outside of work (family and free time)? Alcohol and drug use represent great vulnerabilities. Relationships can also result in vulnerabilities (as well as strengths)
Working conditions	Are there proper work contracts for everyone? Is there access to emergency funds? Insurances?
Recruiting people	Do you have proper procedures for recruiting personnel or collaborators or members? Do you have a specific security approach for your occasional volunteers (such as students, for example) or visitors to your organization?
Working with people or with interface organizations	Is your work done directly with people? Do you know these people well? Do you work with an organization as an interface for your work with people?
Taking care of witness or victims we work with	Do we assess the risk of victims and witnesses, etc, when we are working on specific cases? Do we have specific security measures when we meet them or when they come to our office? If they receive threats, how do we react?
Neighbourhood and social surroundings	Are defenders well socially integrated in the local area? Do some social groups see defenders´ work as good or harmful? Are defenders surrounded by potentially hostile people (neighbours as informers, for example)?
Mobilization capacity	Are defenders able to mobilize people for public activities?

COMPONENTS OF VULNERABILITIES AND CAPACITIES	INFORMATION NEEDED TO ASSESS THE VULNERABILITIES OR CAPACITIES OF THOSE COMPONENTS
PSYCHOLOGICAL COMPONENTS (GROUP/INDIVIDUALS)	
ABILITY TO MANAGE STRESS AND FEAR	Do key individuals, or the group as a whole, feel confident about their work? Do people clearly express feelings of unity and joint purpose (in both words and action)? Are stress levels undermining good communications and interpersonal relationships?
DEEP FEELINGS OF PESSIMISM OR PERSECUTION	Are feelings of depression and loss of hope being clearly expressed (in both words and action)?
WORK RESOURCES	
ABILITY TO UNDERSTAND WORK CONTEXT AND RISK	Do defenders have access to accurate information about their working environment, other stakeholders and their interests? Are defenders able to process that information and get an understanding of threats, vulnerabilities and capacities?
ABILITY TO DEFINE ACTION PLANS	Can defenders define and, in particular, implement action plans? Are there previous examples of this?
ABILITY TO OBTAIN ADVICE FROM WELL INFORMED SOURCES	Can the group obtain reliable advice? From the right sources? Can the group make independent choices about which sources to use? Do you have access to particular organisations or membership status that enhances your protection capacities?
PEOPLE AND AMOUNT OF WORK	Do the people or personnel available match the amount of work needed? Can you plan field visits in teams (at least two people)?
FINANCIAL RESOURCES	Do you have enough financial resources for your security? Can you manage cash in a safe way?
KNOWLEDGE ABOUT LANGUAGES AND AREAS	Do you know the languages needed for the work in this area? Do you know the area properly? (roads, villages, public phones, health centres, etc.)
ACCESS TO NATIONAL AND INTERNATIONAL CONTACTS AND MEDIA	
ACCESS TO NATIONAL AND INTERNATIONAL NETWORKS	Do defenders have national and international contacts? To visiting delegations, embassies, other governments, etc? To community leaders, religious leaders, other people of influence? Can you issue urgent actions via other groups?
ACCESS TO MEDIA AND ABILITY TO OBTAIN RESULTS FROM THEM	Do defenders have access to media (national, international)? To other media (independent media)? Do defenders know how to manage media relations properly?

A risk scales: Another way to understand risk

A scales provides another way to understand this concept of risk: This is something we migth call ... a "risk-meter". If we put two boxes with our threats and vulnerabilities on one of the plates of the scales, and another box with our capacities on the other plate, we will see how our risk gets increased or reduced:

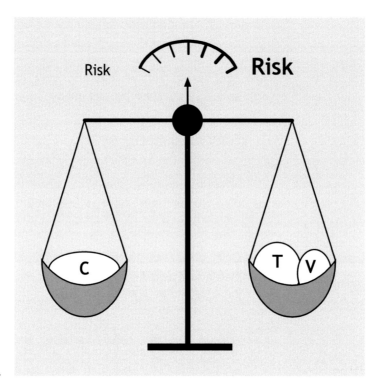

Fig. 1

The more threats and vulnerabilities we have, the more risk we face:

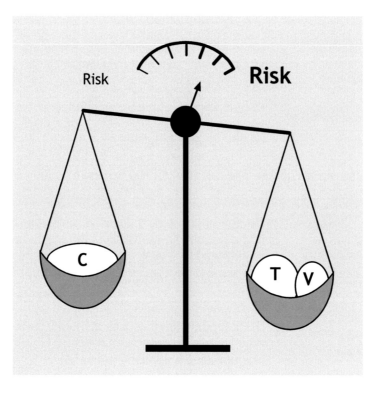

Fig. 2

The more capacities we have, the less risk we face. And for reducing the risk, we can reduce our threats and our vulnerabilities, as well as increase our capacities.

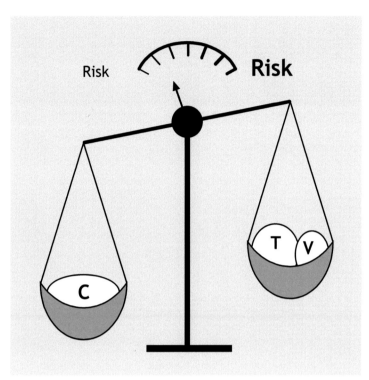

Fig. 3

But ... Look at what happens if we have some big threats: Never mind we try to increase our capacities at that very moment: The scales will show a high level of risk anyway!

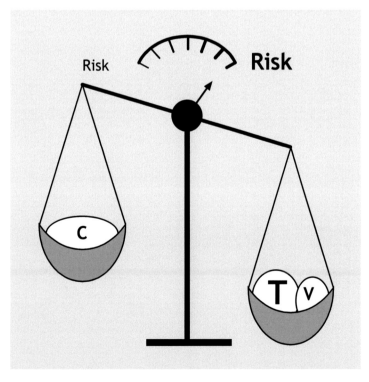

Fig. 4

Understanding and assessing threats

Purpose

To get an in-depth understanding of threats and how to respond to threats.

Threats assessment: Understanding threats in depth

The repression of human rights defenders is all about psychology. Threats are widely used to make defenders feel vulnerable, anxious, confused and helpless. Ultimately, repression also seeks to break organisations and make defenders lose trust in their leaders and colleagues. Defenders have to tread a fine line between careful and proper management of threats and maintaining a sense of safety in our work. This is also the main objective of this chapter.

In Chapter 2, threats were defined as "the possibility that someone will harm somebody else's physical or moral integrity or property, through purposeful, often violent action". We also talked about **possible** threats (when a defender close to your work is threatened and there is reason to believe you might be threatened next), and **declared** threats (receiving a death threat, for example). We will now look at how to deal with **declared threats.**

A declared threat is **a declaration or indication of an intention to inflict damage, punish or hurt, usually in order to achieve something**. Human rights defenders receive threats because of the impact their work is having, and most threats have a clear objective to either stop what the defender is doing or to force him or her to do something.

A threat always has a **source**, i.e. the person or group who has been affected by the defender's work and articulates the threat. A threat also has an **objective** which is linked to the impact of the defender's work, and a **means of expression**, i.e. how it becomes known to the defender.

Threats are tricky. We might say with a certain amount of irony that threats are "ecological", because they aim to achieve major results with a minimum investment of energy. A person making a threat has chosen to do that, rather than take action - a higher investment of energy. Why? There may be a number of reasons why, and it is worth mentioning them here:

☐ The person making the threat has the capacity to act but is to some extent concerned about the political cost of acting openly against a human rights defender. Anonymous threats can be issued for the same reason.

☐ The person making the threat has a limited capacity to act and intends to achieve the same aim by hiding his or her lack of capacity behind a threat. This limited capacity may only be temporary due to other priorities, or permanent, but in both cases things may change and lead to direct action against the defender later on.

A threat is a personal experience, and always has an effect. Or, in other words, threats always affect people in some way. One defender once said that: "Threats achieve some effect, even only due to the fact that we are talking about threats". In fact, any threat can have a double impact: emotionally, and in terms of security. We will concentrate on security here, but we should not forget the emotional side of every threat.

We know that a threat is usually linked to the impact of our work. Receiving a threat therefore represents feedback on how your work is affecting someone else. If you look at it in this way, a threat is an invaluable source of information, and should be analysed carefully.

"Making" vs. "posing" a threat

People issue threats against human rights defenders for many reasons, and only some have the intention or capacity to commit a violent act. However, some individuals can represent a serious threat without ever articulating it. This distinction between *making* and *posing* a threat is important:

- Some people who **make** threats ultimately **pose** a threat.
- Many people who **make** threats **do not pose** a threat.
- Some people who **never make** threats **do pose** a threat.

A threat is only credible if it suggests that the person behind it has the capacity to act against you. It has to demonstrate a minimum level of force or have a menacing element designed to provoke fear.

The person behind the threat can demonstrate his or her capacity to act quite simply, for example by leaving a written threat inside a locked car, even when you have left it parked for just a few minutes, or by phoning just after you have arrived home, letting you know you are being watched.

People can try to instil fear in you by introducing symbolic elements into threats, for example by sending you an invitation to your own funeral or putting a dead animal on your doorstep or on your bed at home.

Many threats show a combination of the above characteristics. It is important to distinguish between them, because some people who send threats pretend to have the capacity to act by using symbolic and frightening elements.

Anyone can make a threat, but not everyone can pose a threat.

At the end of the day, you need to know whether the threat can be put into action. If you are reasonably sure that this is unlikely, your approach will be completely different than if you think a threat has some basis in reality.

The two main objectives when assessing a threat are:

◆ To get as much information as possible about the purpose and source of the threat (both will be linked to the impact of your work).

◆ To reach a reasonable conclusion about whether the threat will be acted on or not.

Five steps to assessing a threat

1 ◆ **Establish the facts surrounding the threat(s).** It's important to know exactly what has happened. This can be done through interviews or by asking questions to key people, and occasionally through relevant reports.

2 ◆ **Establish whether there is a pattern of threats over time.** If several threats are made in a row (as often happens) it is important to look for patterns, such as the means used to threaten, the times when threats appear, symbols, information passed on in writing or verbally, etc. It is not always possible to establish such patterns, but they are important for making a proper threat assessment.

3 ◆ **Establish the objective of the threat.** As a threat usually has a clear objective linked to the impact of your work, following the thread of this impact may help you establish what the threat is intended to achieve.

4 ◆ **Establish who is making the threat.** (This can only be done by going through the first three steps first.) Try to be as specific as possible. For example, you could say that "the government" is threatening you. But since any government is a complex actor, it is more useful to find out which part of the government may be behind the threats. Actors such as "security forces" and "guerrilla groups" are also complex actors. Remember that even a signed threat could be false. This can be a useful way for the person making the threats to avoid political costs and still achieve the aim of provoking fear in a defender and trying to prevent him or her from working.

5 ◆ **Make a reasonable conclusion about whether or not the threat can be put into action.** Violence is conditional. You can never be completely sure that a threat will – or will never - be carried out. Making predictions about violence is about stating that, given certain circumstances, a specific risk exists that a particular person or group will act violently against a particular target.

Defenders are not fortune tellers and cannot pretend to know what is going to happen. However, you can come to a reasonable conclusion about whether or not a given threat is likely to be put into action. You may not have gained enough information about the threat through the previous four steps and may therefore not reach a conclusion. You may also have different opinions about how "real" the threat is. In any case, you have to proceed on the basis of the worst case scenario.

For example:

Death threats have been made against a human rights worker. The group analyses the threats and reach two opposing conclusions, both based on good reasoning. Some say the threat is a total fake, while others people see worrying signals about its feasibility. At the end of the meeting, the group decides to assume the worst case scenario, i.e. that the threat is feasible, and take security measures accordingly.

This threat assessment progresses from solid facts (step 1) to increasingly speculative reasoning. Step 2 involves some interpretation of the facts, and this increases further through steps 3 to 5. There are good reasons for following the order of the steps. Going directly to step 2 or 4, for example, will miss out the more solid information arising from the previous steps.

Maintaining and closing a threat case

A threat or security incident can alarm a group of defenders, but it is usually difficult to maintain this feeling of alarm until the threat has passed. Because of the constant outside pressure on defenders in their work, ringing organisational alarm bells too often could lead the group to lose interest and come off their guard.

Raising a group alarm should only happen based on reliable evidence and should be focused on a specific anticipated event. It must be designed to motivate group members to act, and call for a specific set of actions to be taken. To be most effective, an alarm should only stimulate a moderate level of motivation: Too low doesn't get people to act, but too high creates emotional overload. If the threat is likely to persist over time, it is essential to debrief people and do follow-up after the initial alarm was raised to correct misinformation, change misguided recommendations, and reinforce the group's trust in their joint efforts.

Finally, if the threat does not materialise, some explanation of why must be provided, and the group should be informed that the threat is lower or has disappeared altogether.

You can consider closing a threat case when the potential attacker is deemed to no longer pose a threat. Ideally, to be sure that you are right to close a case, you should be able to explain why first. Questions should also be asked about changed circumstances which could trigger the person behind the threats to move towards violent action.

Reacting to threats in security terms

☐ A threat can be considered a security incident. To find out more about responding to security incidents, turn to Chapter 4.

☐ An assessment of declared threats can lead you to think that you could be attacked. Please see Chapter 5, on preventing attacks.

Security incidents: definition and analysis

Purpose

Learning how to recognise and respond to security incidents.

What is a security incident?

Put simply, a security incident can be defined as **any fact or event which you think could affect your personal or organizational security.**

Examples of security incidents could include seeing the same, suspicious vehicle parked outside your office or home over a number of days; the telephone ringing at night with nobody at the other end; somebody asking questions about you in a nearby town or village, a break-in to your house, etc.

But not everything you notice will constitute a security incident. You should therefore **register** it, by writing it down, and then **analyse** it, ideally with colleagues, to establish if it really could affect your security. At this point you can **react** to the incident. The sequence of events is as follows:

> You notice something ⇨ you realise it might be a security incident ⇨ you register it / share it ⇨ you analyse it ⇨ you establish that it is a security incident ⇨ you react appropriately.

If the matter is pressing, this sequence should still take place, just much more quickly than usual to avoid delay (see below).

How to distinguish between security incidents and threats:

If you are waiting for a bus and somebody standing next to you threatens you because of your work, this - apart from being a threat - constitutes a security incident. But if you discover that your office is being watched from a police car at the opposite side of the street, or your mobile phone is stolen, these are security incidents, but not necessarily threats. Remember: threats have an objective (see Chapter 2), and incidents just happen.

All threats are security incidents, but not all security incidents are threats.

Why are security incidents so important?

Security incidents are crucial to handling your security because **they provide vital information about the impact your work is having, and about possible action which may be planned or carried out against you.** Likewise, such incidents allow you to change your behaviour or activities and avoid places which could be dangerous, or more dangerous than normal. Security incidents can therefore be seen as indicators of the local security situation. If you couldn't detect such changes it would be difficult to take appropriate and timely action to stay safe.

For instance, you may realize that you are under surveillance after noticing several security incidents: Now you can take action about surveillance.

> Security incidents represent "the minimum unit" of
> security measurement and indicates the
> resistance/pressure on your work.
> Do not let them go unnoticed!

When and how do you notice security incidents?

This depends on how obvious the incident is. If it could potentially go unnoticed, your ability to recognise it depends on your security training and experience and your level of awareness.

> The greater your awareness and training,
> the fewer incidents will escape your attention.

Security incidents are sometimes overlooked or briefly noticed and then brushed to one side, or people sometimes overreact to what they perceive as security incidents.

Why a security incident may go unnoticed?

An example:

A defender experiences a security incident, but the organisation s/he works with does not react at all. This could be because...

- the defender isn't aware that a security incident took place.
- the defender is aware of it but dismisses it as unimportant.
- the defender hasn't informed the organisation (s/he forgot, doesn't believe it necessary, or decide to keep quiet because it happened because of a mistake on their part).
- the organisation, having done a team evaluation of the incident after the defender registered it in the incident book, does not judge action necessary.

Why do people sometimes overreact to security incidents?

For example:

A colleague might be constantly telling stories about some security incident or other, but on further examination they prove not to have substance or merit the definition. The actual security incident in this instance is the fact that your colleague has a problem which makes him/her see non-existent security incidents. S/he might be feeling very afraid, or suffering from stress, and should be offered support to resolve the problem.

Do not forget that it is too common that security incidents are overlooked or dismissed: Be careful about this!

Dealing with security incidents

You can deal with security incidents in three basic steps:

1 ◆ **Register them.** Every security incident noticed by a defender must be registered, either in a simple, personal notebook or one accessible to the whole group.

2 ◆ **Analyse them**. All registered security incidents should be properly analysed straight away or on a regular basis. It is better to analyse them as a team rather than individually because this minimises the risk of missing something. Someone should be put in charge of making sure this is done.

Decisions must also be made about whether or not to maintain confidentiality about specific incidents (such as threats). Is it ethical and realistic to keep a threat hidden from colleagues and other people you work with? No single rule applies to every situation, but it is often best to be as open as possible in terms of sharing information and addressing logistical concerns, as well as fears.

3 ◆ **React to them.** Given that security incidents give feedback on the impact of your work, they could lead to the following:

- ◆ Reaction to the incident itself.
- ◆ **Feedback**, in security terms, about how you work, your work **plans** or your work **strategy**.

Example

of an incident which provides feedback on working more securely:

For the third time somebody from your organisation has had problems passing through a police checkpoint because they frequently forget to carry the necessary documents. You therefore decide to compile a checklist which all staff members must consult before leaving the city. You might also change the route for these types of journeys.

Example
of an incident providing feedback on how you plan for security:

At the same police checkpoint, you are detained for half an hour and told that your work is poorly regarded. Thinly veiled threats are made. When you ask for an explanation at police headquarters, the scene is repeated. You call a team meeting to revise your work plans, because it seems clear that changes have to be made in order to continue working. You then plan a series of meetings with Interior Ministry civil servants, change some aspects of your plans and arrange weekly meetings to monitor the situation.

Example
of an incident which provides feedback for your security strategy:

When you start work as defenders in a new area, you immediately receive death threats and one of your colleagues is physically assaulted. You did not anticipate such opposition to your work, nor provide for it in your global strategy. You will therefore have to change your strategy in order to develop tolerance of your work locally and deter further attacks and threats. To do this you have to suspend your work for a while, withdraw from the area and reconsider the entire project.

Reacting *urgently* to a security incident

There are many ways of responding promptly to a security incident. The following steps have been formulated in terms of when and how to react from the moment a security incident is reported, while it is happening, and after it is over.

Step 1. Reporting the incident.

☐ What is happening/has happened (try to focus on the actual facts)?

☐ Where and when did it take place?

☐ Who was involved (if it can be established)?

☐ Was there any injury or damage to individuals or property?

Step 2. Decide when to react. There are two possibilities:

☐ An **immediate reaction** is required to attend to people with injuries or stop an attack.

☐ A **rapid reaction** (in the next few hours or even days) is necessary to prevent possible new security incidents from arising.

☐ **A follow up action** (in several days or weeks or even months): If the situation has stabilised, an immediate or rapid reaction may not be necessary. However, any security incident that requires an immediate or rapid reaction must be followed by a follow up action in order to restore or review your working environment.

Step 3. Decide how to react and what your objectives are.

☐ If the reaction has to be immediate, the objectives are clear: Attend to injuries and/or prevent another attack.

☐ If the reaction has to be quick, the objectives will be established by a crisis team (or similar) and **focus on restoring the necessary security for those affected by the incident.**

Subsequent reactions will take place through the organisation's normal decision-making channels, with the objective of restoring a safe working environment externally, as well as re-establishing internal organisational procedures and improving subsequent reactions to security incidents.

Any reaction also has to take into account the security and protection of other people or organisations or institutions with which you have a working relationship.

Establish your objectives before taking action.
Prompt action is important, but knowing why are
you taking action is more important. By first establishing
what you want to achieve (objectives), you can decide how
to achieve it (course of action).

For instance:

If a defenders´ group has news that one of their colleagues has not duly arrived to her destination in a town, they may start a reaction by calling a hospital and calling their contacts in other NGOs and a nearby UN Office and police. But before starting those calls, it is very important to establish what you want to achieve and what you are going to say. Otherwise you may generate an unnecessary alarm (imagine that the defender was just delayed because they missed a bus and forgot to call the office) or a reaction opposite to the one intended.

Preventing and reacting to attacks

Purpose

Assessing the likelihood of different kinds of attacks taking place.

Preventing possible direct attacks against defenders.

Carrying out counter surveillance.

Attacks against human rights defenders

Violence is a process, as well as an act. A violent attack against a defender does not take place in a vacuum. Careful analysis of attacks often shows that they are the culmination of conflicts, disputes, threats and mistakes which have developed and can be traced over time.

Attacks against defenders are the product of at least three interacting factors:

1 • **The individual who takes violent action.** Attacks on defenders are often the product of of processes of thought and behaviour we can understand and learn from even if they are illegitimate.

2 • **Background and triggers which lead the attacker to see violence as an option.** Most people who attack defenders see attacking as a way of reaching a goal or solving a personal problem.

3 • **A setting** that facilitates the violence, allows it to take place or does not stop it.

Who, then, is a danger to defenders?

Generally, anyone who thinks that attacking a defender is a desirable, acceptable, or potentially effective way to achieve a goal can be considered a potential attacker. The threat increases if s/he also has, or can develop, the capacity to attack a defender.

Some attacks are preceded by threats, and some are not. However, the behaviour of individuals planning a targeted violent attack often shows subtle signs, since they need to gather information about the right time to attack, plan how to get to their target, and how to escape.

> The threat can decrease
> with changes in the potential attacker's
> capacity to stage an attack,
> their attitude towards
> how acceptable an attack is,
> or how likely s/he is
> to be caught and punished.

It is therefore vital to detect and analyse any signs indicating a possible attack. This involves:

- Determining the likelihood of a threat being carried out (see Chapter 3).
- Identifying and analysing security incidents.

Security incidents which involve surveillance of defenders or their workplace are aimed at gathering information. This information isn't always intended for use in an attack, but it is important to try and establish whether it is or not (see Chapter 4).

Surveillance of staff or offices is intended to acquire information about them and can be used for a number of purposes:

- To establish what activities are carried out, when and with/by whom.
- To use this information later to attack individuals or organisations.
- To gather the information necessary to carry out an attack.
- To gather information for a legal action action or other harassment (without direct violence).
- To intimidate your supporters or other people who work with you, or provide you with information to stop doing so.

It is important to remember that surveillance is usually necessary in order to carry out an attack, but doesn't in itself constitute an attack. Also, not all surveillance is followed by an attack. Targeted violence does sometimes occur in situations when an attacker suddenly sees an opportunity to strike, but even then some level of preparation has usually been carried out first.

There is little information available to help you recognise an attack being prepared. The absence of studies on this subject contrasts sharply with the large number of attacks against defenders. However, the studies which do exist offer some interesting insights[1].

---

[1] Claudia Samayoa and Jose Cruz (Guatemala) and Jaime Prieto (Colombia) have produced interesting studies on attacks against human rights defenders. Mahony and Eguren (1997) also carried out an analysis of such attacks.

❑ **Attacking a defender isn't easy and requires resources.** Surveillance is needed to establish an individual's movements and the best location for attacking. Getting to the target and making an effective, quick escape is also vital. (However, if the environment is highly favourable to the attacker, attacks are easier to carry out).

❑ **People who attack defenders usually show a degree of consistency.** The majority of attacks are aimed at defenders who are heavily involved in issues affecting the attackers. In other words, usually attacks are not random or aimless, but respond to the interests of the attackers.

❑ **Geographical factors matter.** For example, attacks on defenders in rural areas are less public and therefore provoke less reaction at law enforcement level and political level than attacks in urban areas. Attacks against NGO headquarters or high profile organisations in urban areas generate an even greater reaction.

❑ **Choices and decisions are made before an attack.** People who are considering an attack against a defenders' organisation must decide whether to attack the leaders or grass-roots members, and choose between a single hit (against a key, possibly high profile person and there-fore at an increased political cost) or a series of attacks (affecting the organisation's membership). The few studies done on attacks against defenders suggest that both strategies are usually applied.

Establishing the feasibility of an attack

To find out how likely an attack is to happen, you need to analyse the relevant factors involved. To establish what those factors are, it is useful to differentiate between different kinds of attacks, i.e. common crime, indirect attacks (being in the wrong place at the wrong time) and direct attacks (targeting), using the three tables on the following pages[2].

---

[2] This classification of attacks includes the same categories as for threats: Please have a look at the chapter on threats for clarification.

Table 1: Establishing the threat level of direct attacks (targeting)

(**PA** stands for potential attackers)

THREAT LEVEL FOR DIRECT ATTACKS (TARGETING)			
FACTORS	LOW THREAT	MEDIUM THREAT	HIGH THREAT
CAPACITY TO ATTACK	PA have limited ability to act in the areas where you work	PA have operational capacity near the areas where you work	Zones where you work under the firm control of PA
FINANCIAL MOTIVE	PA do not need your equipment or cash for their activities	Interest in your equipment, cash, or other forms of financial gain (i.e. kidnapping)	PA in clear need of equipment or cash
POLITICAL AND MILITARY MOTIVE	None - your work has nothing to do with their objectives	Partial interest - your work limits their political and military objectives	Your work clearly hampers their objectives, benefits their opponents, etc.
RECORD OF PREVIOUS ATTACKS	None or rare	Occasional cases	Many previous cases
ATTITUDES OR INTENTIONS	Sympathetic or indifferent attitude	Indifferent Occasional threats Frequent warnings	Aggressive, with clear and present threats
SECURITY FORCES' CAPACITY TO DETER ATTACKS	Existing	Low	None, or security forces collaborate with PA
YOUR LEVEL OF POLITICAL CLOUT AGAINST PA	Good	Medium to low	Limited (depending on circumstances) or none

Example

of the threat level for direct attacks (targeting):

The PA control the areas in which you work, but they do not have any financial motive for attacking you. Your work only partially limits their political and military objectives, and there are no precedents of similar attacks in the city. Their attitude is indifferent, and they do clearly not want to attract any national attention or pressure by attacking you.

The threat level for direct attacks in this scenario is considered to be low to medium.

Table 2: Establishing the threat level for crime

(CO stands for criminal offenders)

LEVEL OF THREAT FOR CRIME			
FACTORS	LOW THREAT	MEDIUM THREAT	HIGH THREAT
MOBILITY AND LOCATION OF CO	CO usually stay in their own areas, away from NGO zones	CO generally enter other areas at night (or operate close to NGO areas)	CO operate anywhere, day or night
AGGRESSIVENESS OF CO	CO avoid confrontation (predominantly commit crime where there is no NGO presence)	CO commit crime in the street (but not in staffed offices)	CO openly commit street robberies and enter premises to commit crime
ACCES TO/USE OF WEAPONS	Unarmed or use non-lethal arms	Crude weapons, including machetes	Firearms, sometimes powerful
SIZE AND ORGANISATION	Operate individually or in pairs	2-4 people operate together	Operate in groups
POLICE RESPONSE AND DETERRENCE	Rapid response, capable of deterrence	Slow response, little success capturing criminals in the act	Police do not usually respond with even a minimum degree of effectiveness
TRAINING AND PROFESSIONALISM OF SECURITY FORCES	Well trained and professional but lacking resources	Regular training, low pay, limited resources	Police are either non-existent or corrupt (cooperate with offenders)
GENERAL SECURITY SITUATION	There is lawlessness but the situation is relatively secure	Lack of security	Rights not observed, absolute impunity

Example

of an assessment of the threat level for crime:

*In this city, criminals operate in different areas in pairs or small groups, sometimes during the day. They are often aggressive and often carry guns. The police does respond, but slowly and ineffectively, and the police force is unprofessional and under-resourced. However, the police leadership is well disciplined. There is a clear lack of security, and if applied to the marginal neighbourhoods of the city, the threat of crime is at its highest given that **all** the indicators are at high level.*

The likelihood of a criminal attack in the centre of a city like this is at a high to medium level.

Table 3: Establishing the threat level for indirect attacks

(**PA** stands for potential attackers)

\LEVEL OF THREAT FOR INDIRECT ATTACKS			
FACTORS	LOW THREAT	MEDIUM THREAT	HIGH THREAT
YOUR KNOWLEDGE OF CONFLICT AREAS	Good	Approximate	You know very little about where combat zones are located
DISTANCE TO CONFLICT AREAS	Your work is far away from these areas	Your work is close to these areas and you occasionally enter them	Your work is carried out in combat zones
MOVEMENT OF CONFLICT AREAS	Conflicts are static, or change slowly and verifiably	They change relatively often	They change continually, making them unpredictable
YOUR KNOWLEDGE OF LOCATION OF AREAS WITH LANDMINES	You have good knowledge or there are no mined areas	Approximate knowledge	Unknown
DISTANCE BETWEEN YOUR WORK PLACE AND AREAS WITH LANDMINES	Your work takes place far away from these areas, or there are none	Your work is close to these areas and you occasionally enter them	Your work takes place in mined areas
COMBAT TACTICS AND ARMS	Discriminate	Discriminate, with occasional use of artillery, ambushes and snipers	Indiscriminate: bombardment, heavy artillery, terrorist or bomb attacks

Example

of an assessment of the threat level for indirect attacks:

In this area, you are familiar with the combat zones, which change slowly and verifiably. Your work is close to the areas where the fighting takes place and you occasionally visit or stay in the combat zones. You are not close to mined areas. The combat tactics used are discriminate and therefore do not affect civilians very often.

Work in this zone carries a low level of risk of indirect attack.

Preventing a possible direct attack

You now know that a threat can decrease with changes in the potential attacker's capacity to stage an attack, their attitude towards how acceptable an attack is, or how likely s/he is to be caught and punished.

To prevent an attack it is therefore necessary to:

◆ Persuade a potential attacker or a person making threats that an attack will involve unacceptable costs and consequences;

◆ Make attacks less feasible.

This type of attack prevention is similar to the analysis covered in Chapter 2 which says that risk is dependent on the defenders' vulnerabilities and capacities. It also said that in order to protect yourselves and reduce risk, you need to take action against the threat, reduce your vulnerabilities and enhance your capacities.

Table 4: Preventing a direct attack – different protection outcomes

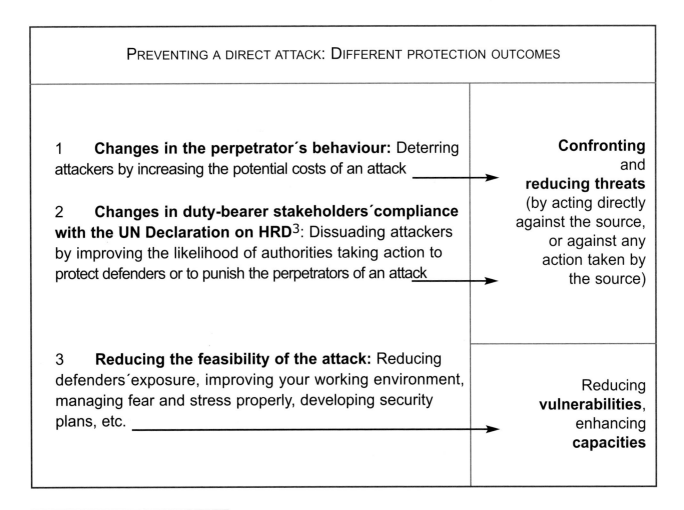

PREVENTING A DIRECT ATTACK: DIFFERENT PROTECTION OUTCOMES	
1 Changes in the perpetrator´s behaviour: Deterring attackers by increasing the potential costs of an attack ⟶ **2 Changes in duty-bearer stakeholders´compliance with the UN Declaration on HRD[3]:** Dissuading attackers by improving the likelihood of authorities taking action to protect defenders or to punish the perpetrators of an attack ⟶	**Confronting** and **reducing threats** (by acting directly against the source, or against any action taken by the source)
3 Reducing the feasibility of the attack: Reducing defenders´exposure, improving your working environment, managing fear and stress properly, developing security plans, etc. ⟶	Reducing **vulnerabilities**, enhancing **capacities**

---

[3] See chapter 1. For example, after a defender denounces threats, either the prosecutor or the police or some other body investigates what has happened and this investigation leads to action against those who are threatening the defender. Well, at least this may be the objective of a reaction to prevent an attack.

When a threat is made and you want to reduce the risk associated with it, it is important to act - not just against the threat itself, but also on the **vulnerabilities** and **capacities** most **closely linked** to the threat. At times of great pressure, when you want to react as quickly as possible, you often act on the vulnerabilities which are easiest to deal with or closest to hand instead of those which are most relevant to the threat.

Be careful: If the risk of attack is high (that is, if the threat is strong and real, and there are several vulnerabilities and fewer capacities), working on vulnerabilities or capacities to reduce the risk makes little sense, because these require time to change and become functional. If the risk is very high (a direct and severe attack is imminent) you can only do three things to avoid it:

a ◆ Immediately and effectively confront the threat, knowing that you can achieve an immediate and specific result which will prevent the attack (Usually it is very difficult to be sure that there will be an immediate and effective result, because reactions take time, and time is precious in this situation)

b ◆ Reduce your exposure to as close to zero as possible, by going into hiding or leaving the area[4].

c ◆ Seeking armed protection, assuming that armed protection is close at hand (immediate), can deter the potential attacker and does not put the defender in more danger in the medium or long term (realistically, such requirements of armed protection are very difficult to fulfil!). Sometimes a Government offers armed escorts to a defender, after national or international pressure; in these cases, accepting or rejecting the escort may have to do with holding the state accountable for the security of defenders, but in no way can a Government say that they are relieved of their responsibilities if the defender does not accept the armed escorts. Private security companies may lead to more risk if they are informally linked to State forces (see chapter 9). And for defenders to carry weapons we must say that it is usually ineffective against an organized attack, and also may make defenders vulnerable if a Government uses it as a pretext to attack them on the basis of fighting terrorism or insurgency.

Threatening situations that can lead to an attack are easier to handle if other relevant actors or stakeholders become involved and work together. Examples include a functioning judicial system; support networks (domestic and international) that can put political pressure on duty-bearer stakeholders; social networks (within or among organisations), personal and family networks, UN/international peacekeepers, etc.

Surveillance and counter-surveillance

Counter-surveillance can help you establish whether you are being watched. It is difficult to find out whether your communications are being intercepted, and for this reason you should always assume that they are[5]. However, it is possible to determine if your movements and offices are being watched.

---

[4] However, there will be occasions where attempting to travel might put someone at greater risk.
[5] For more information on securing communications see Capter 12.

Who could be watching you?

People who are usually in your area, such as doormen or porters in buildings, travelling sales people who work close to the building entrance, people in nearby vehicles, visitors, etc., could potentially all be watching your movements. People do surveillance for money; because they are being pressurised to do it; because of their sympathies, or due to a combination of these factors. Those behind the surveillance can also place collaborators or members of their organisation in your area.

People can also watch you from a distance. In this case they are almost always members of an organisation and probably use the tactic of watching without wishing to be seen. This means keeping a certain distance, various people taking turns and watching from different locations, using different vehicles, etc.

How to know if you are being watched

You can find out if you're being observed by watching those who could be watching you, and by adopting the following rules (without, of course, becoming paranoid):

□ If you have reason to think that somebody might want to watch you, you should be mindful of the movements of people in your area and changes in their attitude, for example, if they start asking about your activities. Remember that women and men can do surveillance, as can old or very young people.

□ If you suspect that you are being followed, it is possible to put in place a counter-surveillance measure involving a third party whom you trust, and who is unknown to those who might be watching you. This third party can watch, in advance and from a good distance, movements which occur when you arrive, leave or go somewhere. Whoever is watching will probably do so from a place where you can always be easily located, including your home, offices and the places where you most often do your work.

For example

Before arriving home you can ask a family member or trusted neighbour to take up a position close by (e.g., changing a car wheel), to check if somebody is awaiting your arrival. The same can be done when leaving your office on foot. If you are using a private vehicle, it will be necessary to have another car leave after yours in order to allow a potential observer time to begin their approach towards you.

The benefit of counter-surveillance is that, at least initially, the person observing you does not realise you know they are there. It should therefore be made clear to anyone involved that it may not be advisable confront the person observing you. They will then realise that you know about their activities, and this could also provoke a violent reaction. It is important to take the utmost care and keep a distance if you are aware of somebody watching you. Once surveillance has been detected, you can take the necessary action recommended in this manual (see Chapter 9).

Most of this counter surveillance advice applies almost exclusively to urban and semi-urban areas. In rural areas the situation is very different, but defenders and communities who live in such areas are more used to being aware of strangers nearby. It is therefore more difficult for somebody who wants to watch you to gain access to inhabitants of a rural area - unless the local population is deeply hostile towards your work.

A note: Building relationship with the security forces monitoring you could be beneficial in some circumstances – and in some circumstances it is not so secret the surveillance, part of the point is to make it visible/intimidating. In some situations defenders cultivate people in the security forces who can then some-times tip them off when surveillance or even an action is planned against them.

When to check if you are being watched

Logic dictates that it is wise to check if you are under surveillance if you have reason to believe that you are - for example, because of security incidents which could be related to surveillance. If your human rights work carries a certain risk, it is a good idea to conduct a simple counter-surveillance exercise from time to time, just in case.

You need also to think about risk you bring to others if you are under surveil-lance – the risk may be greater for a witness/family member of a victim you are meeting than for you – think about where it would be most secure for them to meet? You may need to warn them that your movements might be under surveillance.

Reacting to attacks

No single rule can be applied to all attacks against defenders. Attacks are also security incidents, and you can find guidelines for how to react to security incidents in Chapter 4.

In any kind of attack there are two essential things to remember:

☐ Think always about security! – both **during** and **after** the attack! (If you are under attack and you have to make a choice between two alternatives, go for the safest one!)

☐ Following an attack, it will be necessary to recover physically and psychologically, take action to solve the situation, and restore a safe work environment for you and your organisation. It is crucial to retain as much detailed information as possible about the attack: What happened, who/how many people were involved, number plates of vehicles, descrip-tions, etc. This can be useful to document the case, and should be compiled as quickly as possible. Keep copies of any documents handed over to the authorities to document the case.

CHAPTER 6

Preparing a security strategy and plan

Purpose

Learning how to draft a security strategy.

Learning how to draw up a security plan.

Human rights defenders working in hostile environments

Too often, defenders work in hostile environments. There are many reasons why. Most relate to the fact that defenders' work may lead them to confront powerful actors who are violating international human rights law, be it government or state authorities, security forces, opposition armed groups or private armed gangs. These actors may retaliate by trying to stop defenders doing their work, through anything from subtle repression of attempts at free expression to declared threats and direct attacks. The actors' level of tolerance depends on the defenders' work - some activities might be deemed acceptable, others not. Often this uncertainty is also deliberate.

Two important considerations should be made here: In many cases, it is only certain elements **within** complex actors (such as those mentioned above) who are hostile towards defenders. For example, some elements within a government may be relatively serious about protecting defenders, while other elements want to attack them. Defenders may also experience more hostility during times of political upheaval, such as elections or other political events.

Defenders' socio-political work space

This manual focuses on the protection and security of human rights defenders working in hostile environments and measures which are focussed on improving their security. There is of course action which can be taken at the socio-political level to improve respect for human rights and the environment for human rights defenders. The campaigning and promotion activities of human rights defenders are often aimed at securing a broader acceptance of human rights within society or more effective action from political actors to ensure human rights are protected. We don't usually think of such activities as about security but when successful they can have a positive impact on protecting human rights defenders' **socio-political work space.**

This socio-political work space can be defined as the **variety of possible actions the defender can take at an acceptable personal risk.** In other words, the defender perceives *"a broad array of possible political actions and associates a certain cost or set of consequences with each action".* The defender perceives some of these consequences as *"acceptable and others as unacceptable, thereby defining the limits of a distinct political space"* .

For instance, a defenders´ group may pursue a human rights case until one of the members of the group receives a death threat. If they perceive they have enough socio-political space, they may decide to make public that they have been threatened, and eventually go on with the case. But if they perceive that their political space is limited, they may reckon that denouncing the threat will have unacceptable costs. They might even decide to drop the case for a while and improve their security capacities in the meantime.

The notion of "acceptable" risk can change over time and varies greatly between individuals or organisations. For some, torture or the death of a family member might be the most unbearable risk. Some defenders believe that being imprisoned is an acceptable risk, as long as it helps to achieve their goals. For others, the threshold might be reached with the first threat.

This political space of activity, in addition to being subjectively defined by those who move within it, is very sensitive to changes in the surrounding national political environment. You therefore have to look at it as a relative and changeable space.

Security and defenders' work space

All security strategies can be summarised in a few words: You want to expand your work space and sustain it in that way. Speaking strictly in security terms, defenders' work space requires at least a minimum level of consent by the main actors in the area - especially by political and military authorities and armed groups who might become affected by defenders' work and decide to act against them.

This consent can be **explicit**, such as a formal permit from the authorities, or **implicit**, for example, in the case of armed groups. Consent will be more solid if the actor can see some benefit resulting from the defenders´ work. It will be lower if the actor perceives related costs. In this case, their level of consent will depend on the political costs carried by an attack on defenders. These issues are especially relevant in armed conflicts where defenders face more than one armed actor. One armed actor might see defenders´ work as helpful to their opponent. Another actor's open acceptance of defenders´ work may therefore lead to hostility by their opponent.

Defenders' work space can be represented by two axes:

□ one representing the extent to which the actor will tolerate or accept your work based on the extent to which your work impacts on the actor's objectives or strategic interests (the tolerance-acceptance continuum).

---

[1] This definition and other key parts of this concept have been taken from Mahony and Eguren (1997), p. 93. They have also developed a model of political space that integrates defenders' work space with the protective accompaniment of defenders.

□ one representing the extent to which you can deter attacks, because of high political costs, expanding to when you can dissuade the actor on rational/moral grounds or even persuade them of political benefits to not attacking you or violating human rights (the deterrence-dissuasion continuum).

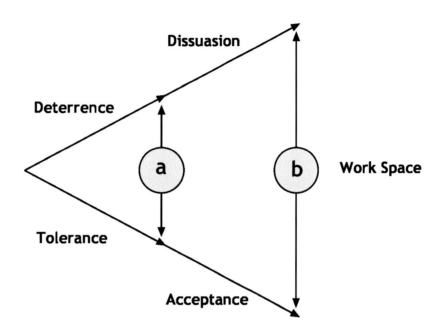

The expansion of your work space can be achieved over time. Achieving acceptance of defenders´ work through a strategy of dissuasion should take into account working for the needs of the population, your image, procedures, integration etc, as represented in space "b". But in areas of armed conflict the space usually remains limited to just that which follows from the armed actors' consent, partially generated as a result of the costs of attacking the defenders (dissuasion), then having the space reduced to "a".

Expanding your work space by increasing tolerance and acceptance

Your work may affect the objectives or strategic interests of someone who does not care much about human rights, leading to a hostile working environment for defenders. In order to gain acceptance, or at least consent, for your work, it is important to limit the confrontation to a necessary minimum. Some suggestions for how to do this:

□ **Provide information and training about the nature and legitimacy of defenders' work.** Government officials and other actors may be more inclined to cooperate if they know and understand your work and your reasons for undertaking it. It is not enough just for higher officials to be aware of what you do, because defenders' daily work usually involves many levels of officials in different government bodies. You should make a continuous effort to inform and train officials at all levels.

□ **Clarify the objectives of defenders' work.** In all conflicts it is useful to clarify and limit the scope and objectives of your work. This will reduce misunderstandings or unnecessary confrontations that can stop defenders achieving their aims.

□ **Limit your work objectives to match the socio-political space of your work.** When defenders' work affects an armed actor's specific strategic interests, the actor may react more violently and with less consideration for his image. Some types of work make defenders more vulnerable than others, so make sure your objectives match your risk situation and protection capacities as much as possible.

□ **Allow space in your strategies for "saving face".** If you have to confront an actor about human rights abuses seek to leave them a way to gain credit for taking action to address the situation

□ **Establish alliances** widely with as many social sectors as possible.

□ **Find a balance** between transparency in your work, to show that legitimate defenders have nothing to hide, and the need to avoid giving out information that could compromise your work or security.

□ **Finally,** remember that the legitimacy and quality of your work are necessary conditions for keeping your work space open, but it may not be enough. You may also need to be able to dissuade potential attackers (see below).

Expanding your work space: Increasing deterrence and dissuasion

Human rights defenders working in hostile environments should be able to conjure up enough political costs to frighten an aggressor into not attacking them: This is called **deterrence**.

It is useful to distinguish between "general" and "immediate" deterrence. **General deterrence** consist of the combined effect of all national and international efforts at protecting defenders, i.e. anything which helps to create a general understanding that attacks against defenders will have negative consequences. This can happen through wide thematic campaigns or training and information about protecting defenders. On the other hand, immediate deterrence sends a specific message to a specific aggressor to keep their attacks away from a specific target. **Immediate deterrence** is necessary when general deterrence fails or is seen to be insufficient, and when protection efforts are focused on specific cases.

Dissuasion is a more inclusive concept. It can be defined as the result of acts which induce an opponent not to carry out a contemplated hostile action. Rational argument, moral appeal, increased cooperation, improved human understanding, distraction, adoption of non-offensive policy and deterrence may all be used to achieve dissuasion. Each of these tactics are used at different times by defenders at the national or international levels. Defenders cannot of course use direct "threats" very often: The strategy is more about reminding others that, depending on their decisions, a series of consequences **could** occur.

Putting deterrence to work

In order to measure whether we have been effective in deterrence, a series of conditions must be met:

1 • **Defenders must clearly specify and communicate to the aggressor what types of actions are unacceptable.** Deterrence will not work if the aggressor does not know which actions will provoke a response.

2 • **The defenders' organisation must articulate its commitment to deterring the aggression in a way that makes the aggressor aware of it.** The organisation must also have a strategy in place for accomplishing the deterrence.

3 • **The defenders' organisation must be capable of carrying out the deterrence, and make the aggressor aware of this.** If a threat of mobilising national or international reaction is not credible, there is no reason to expect it to have a protective effect.

4 • **Defenders must know who the aggressor is.** Hit squads often work in the dark of night and rarely claim responsibility. This therefore often boils down to analysing who might benefit from an attack. In order to improve the effectiveness of a national or international reaction, an assumption of "state responsibility", although correct, requires more specific information about which factions within the state apparatus are behind the attack.

5 • **The aggressor must have seriously considered attacking and then decided not to carry it out** because the costs - due to the defenders' commitment - would be greater than the benefits.

It is difficult for defenders to dissuade an aggressor who will remain unaffected by a commitment to deter: This happens when governments can be punished by the international community, but cannot in turn punish the actual human rights violator. For example, private armies can be outside the government's reach or don't share its interests. In such cases, the aggressor may even benefit from attacking human rights defenders, because attacks will put the government in a difficult position and harm its image.

Defenders will never know in advance if their "deterrence commitment" is strong enough to dissuade a potential attack. The aggressor may expect benefits that defenders are not aware of. Assessing the situation as carefully as possible is a permanent challenge and may even be impossible due to lack of critical information. Defenders' organisations must therefore develop extremely flexible fallback plans and the ability to respond rapidly to unexpected events.

Drafting a security plan

It should not be difficult to draft a security plan. Here is a process in just a few steps:

1 • **The components of the plan.** A security plan is aimed at reducing your risk. It will therefore have at least three objectives, based on your risk assessment:

- Reducing the level of threat you are experiencing.
- Reducing your vulnerabilities.
- Enhancing your capacities.

It could be useful if your security plan also includes:

- Preventive plans or protocols, to ensure routine work is done within security standards, for example, how to prepare a public allegation or a visit to a remote area.

- Emergency plans for dealing with specific problems, for example, a detention or a disappearance.

2 • **Responsibilities and resources for implementing the plan.** To ensure that the plan is implemented, security routines must be integrated into daily work activities:

- Include context assessment and security points routinely in your agendas.
- Register and analyse security incidents.
- Allocate responsibilities.
- Allocate resources, i.e. time and funds, for security.

3 • **Drafting the plan - how to begin.** If you have done a risk assessment for a defender or organisation, you might have a long list of vulnerabilities, several kinds of threats and a number of capacities. You can't realistically cover everything at the same time. So where to begin? It's very easy:

- **Select a few threats.** Prioritise the threats you have listed, be it actual or potential ones, using one of these criteria: The most serious threat - clear death threats, for example; OR the most probable and serious threat - if organisations similar to yours have been attacked, that is a clear potential threat for you; OR the threat which corresponds most with your vulnerabilities - because you are more at risk of that specific threat.

- **List the vulnerabilities you have which correspond with the threats you have listed.** These vulnerabilities should be addressed first, but remember that not all vulnerabilities correspond with all threats. For example, if you receive a death threat, it may not be very useful to start securing the cupboards in your office in the city centre (unless you can be easily attacked in the office, which is usually not the case). It may be more useful to reduce your exposure while commuting from home to the office or on weekends. Securing the cupboards isn't unimportant, but that in itself probably won't reduce your vulnerability to the death threat.

- **List the capacities you have which correspond with the threats you have listed.**

You are now in a position to address the selected threats, vulnerabilities and capacities in your security plan, and can be reasonably sure that you will be able to reduce your risk from the right starting point.

Please note that this is an ad hoc way of drafting a security plan. There are more "formal" ways to do it, but this method is straightforward and makes sure you take care of the most urgent security issues - provided your risk assessment is correct - and end up with an "alive" and "real" plan at the end, and that's the important part of security. *(Please see the end of this Chapter for a detailed list of possible security plan components which you can also use when assessing your risks).*

Coping with security challenges: Step by step security management

Security management never ends and is always partial and selective. This is because:

☐ There are limits to the amount of information you can deal with - not all factors affecting security can be grouped and treated simultaneously.

☐ It is a complex process - time and effort are necessary to create awareness, develop consensus, train people, deal with staff turnover, implement activities, etc.

Security management is pragmatic

Security management can rarely attempt a comprehensive, long-term overview. Its contribution lies in the ability to prevent attacks and highlight the need for organisational strategies to cope with these. This may not seem very ambitious, but we must not forget that too few resources are usually allocated for security!

When reviewing a defender's or an organisation's security practices you may discover some sort of guidelines, plans, measures or patterns of behaviour already in place. There will be conflicting forces involved, ranging from stereotypical ideas about security practices to a reluctance to increase existing workloads by incorporating new security activities.

Security practice is typically a fragmented and intuitive work in progress. Security management should aim to make step by step changes to improve performance. Security rules and procedures tend to emerge from parts of an organisation covering specific areas of work, such as logistics or a field team especially concerned with its security, a manager under pressure by donor concerns about security, etc.

Step by step security management opens the door to informal processes and allows space for new practices to take root. Sudden events, such as security incidents, will prompt urgent, short-term decisions that, if properly managed, will shape longer term security practices for the whole organisation.

Implementing a security plan

Security plans are important, but they are not easy to implement. Implementation is much more than a technical process - it is an organisational process. This means looking for entry points and opportunities, as well barriers and problems.

A security plan must be implemented on at least three levels:

1 ◦ The **individual** level. Each individual has to follow the plan in order for it to work.

2 ◦ The **organisational** level. The organisation as a whole has to follow the plan.

3 ◦ The **inter-organisational** level. Some level of cooperation between organisations is usually involved to maintain security.

Examples of entry points and opportunities when implementing a security plan:

☐ Several minor security incidents have taken place in your own or another organisation and some staff members are worried about it.

☐ General security concerns exist because of the situation in the country.

☐ New staff arrive and can be trained to start good security practices more easily.

☐ Another organisation offers you security training.

Examples of problems and barriers to implementing a security plan:

☐ Some people think more security measures will lead to an even greater workload.

☐ Others think the organisation already has good enough security.

☐ "We haven't got time for this stuff!"

☐ "OK, let's make extra time to discuss security on Saturday morning, but that's it!"

☐ "We need to take better care of the people we intend to help, not ourselves."

Ways of improving the implementation of a security plan

☐ **Take advantage of opportunities and entry points** to face problems and break through barriers.

☐ **Proceed step by step.** There's no point in pretending that everything can be done at once.

☐ **Emphasise the importance of security to core work on behalf of victims.** Stress that the security of witnesses and family members is critical to the effectiveness of core work and that this can best be managed by integrating good security practices into all areas of work. Use examples in training/discussion that demonstrate the potential negative impact of lax security on witnesses and victims.

❑ A plan drafted by two "experts" and presented to a whole organisation is likely to fall flat on its face. In security, **participation is key.**

❑ **A plan must be realistic and feasible.** A long list of things to do before every field trip will not work. Keep to the bare minimum necessary to ensure security. This is another reason to involve those who really do the work - for example, people who usually go on field trips.

❑ **The plan is not a one-off document** - it must be reviewed and updated all the time.

❑ **The plan must not be seen as "more work", but as "a better way to work".** People must be made to see the benefits, for example, by avoiding duplicate reporting. Make sure field trip reports have a security dimension, make security issues part of normal team meetings, integrate security aspects into other training, etc.

❑ **Emphasise that security is not a personal choice.** Individual decisions, attitudes and behaviour that impacts on security can have consequences for the security of witnesses, family members of victims and colleagues. There needs to be a collective commitment to implementing good security practices.

❑ **Time and resources must be allocated** to implementing the plan, as security cannot be improved by using people's free time. In order to be seen as "important", security activities must be placed alongside other "important" activities.

❑ **Everyone must be seen to follow the plan,** especially managers and those responsible for other people's work. There must be consequences for individuals who persistently refuse to abide by the plan.

Possible elements to include in a security plan

This "menu" lists detailed suggestions for elements to include in a security plan. After doing a risk assessment, you can pick and mix these ideas to complete your security plan.

❑ The organization's mandate, mission and general objectives.

❑ An organizational statement on security policy.

❑ Security should cut across all aspects of daily work: Context assessment, risk assessment and incident analysis, as well as security evaluation.

❑ How to ensure that all staff are properly trained in security to the necessary level and that people's security responsibilities are passed on when they leave the organisation.

❑ Allocation of responsibilities: Who is expected to do what in which situations?

☐ How to handle a security crisis: Setting up a crisis committee or working group, delegating responsibility for handling the media, communicating with relatives, etc.

☐ Organizational security responsibilities: Planning, follow-up, insurance, civil responsibility, etc.

☐ Individual security responsibilities: Always reducing risk, how to handle free time or leisure activities, reporting and recording security incidents, sanctions (some of these points could be included in work contracts, if applicable).

☐ Organizational policies on:

1- Rest, free time and stress management. 2- Serious incidents, such as kidnapping, disappearance, personal injury, etc. 3- The security of witnesses. 4- Health and accident prevention. 5- Links with authorities, security forces and armed groups. 6- Information management and storage, handling confidential documents and information. 7- Your own image in relation to religious, social and cultural values. 8- Security management in offices and homes (including for visitors).

☐ Prevention plans and protocols on:

1- Preparing field trips. 2- Handling cash or valuables. 3- Communication means and protocol. 4- Vehicle maintenance. 5- Landmines. 6- Reducing the risk of getting involved in common crime, armed incidents or sexual attacks. 7- Reducing the risk of accidents when travelling or in risky areas.

☐ Plans and protocols for reacting to security crises, such as:

1- Medical and psychological emergencies (also in the field). 2- Attacks, including sexual attacks. 3- Robbery. 4- Reacting when a person does not show up when supposed to. 5- Arrest or detention. 6- Kidnapping. 7- Fire and other accidents. 8- Evacuation. 9- Natural disasters. 10- Legal or illegal searches or break-ins into offices or homes. 11- If a person comes under fire. 12- If someone is killed. 13- If there is a coup d´etat.

CHAPTER 7

Assessing organisational security performance: the security wheel

Purpose

Examining the way you manage security.

Evaluating the extent to which security is integrated into human rights defenders' work.

The security wheel

Let's begin with the easy bit: In order to turn properly, a wheel must be completely round. Up to this point there is no argument. But what happens if some of the spokes are longer than others? The wheel would not be completely round and would therefore not function properly.

Something similar happens with security management in a group or organisation. If the main security components are not developed at the same time, the overall security strategy can not be expected to work well. On this basis, you can sketch a so-called "security wheel". you can use it to examine the way you manage security, and evaluate the extent to which security is integrated into a group of defenders' work.

This evaluation can be done as a group. You can list a range of ideas about why particular parts of the wheel have not been sufficiently developed, and suggest lots of ways of solving these problems. When you have listed the possible solutions, you can get to work and choose the ones you want to use.

Once you have completed this evaluation of your security wheel, hold on to the result and the diagram. When you repeat the exercise in a few months' time, you can then compare your old and new diagrams and see point by point if things have improved or not.

The components of the security wheel

The security wheel has eight spokes, or components:

□ **On-the-job experience**: Practical accumulated knowledge of security and protection. Your point of departure and arrival.

□ **Training**. You can get security training on a course or through your own initiative during your daily work.

□ **Awareness of and attitude towards security**: Relates to whether each individual and the whole organisation really see protection and security as necessities and are prepared to work towards ensuring them.

□ **Planning**: Planning capacity for security and work. Planning for protection.

□ **Assignment of responsibilities**: Who is responsible for which aspects of security and protection? And in emergencies?

□ **Degree of ownership of security rules / compliance**: To what degree are people following the security rules and procedures?

□ **Analysing and reacting to security incidents**: To what degree are security incidents analysed? Does the organisation respond appropriately?

□ **Evaluating security and protection management**: If your daily work, as well as reactions to security incidents, are evaluated, this will contribute to individuals' and the organisations' knowledge and experience.

Now that you are more familiar with the components of the security wheel, try to construct a diagram adding more information. It could look something like this:

THE SECURITY WHEEL AND ITS EIGHT COMPONENT PARTS, OR SPOKES

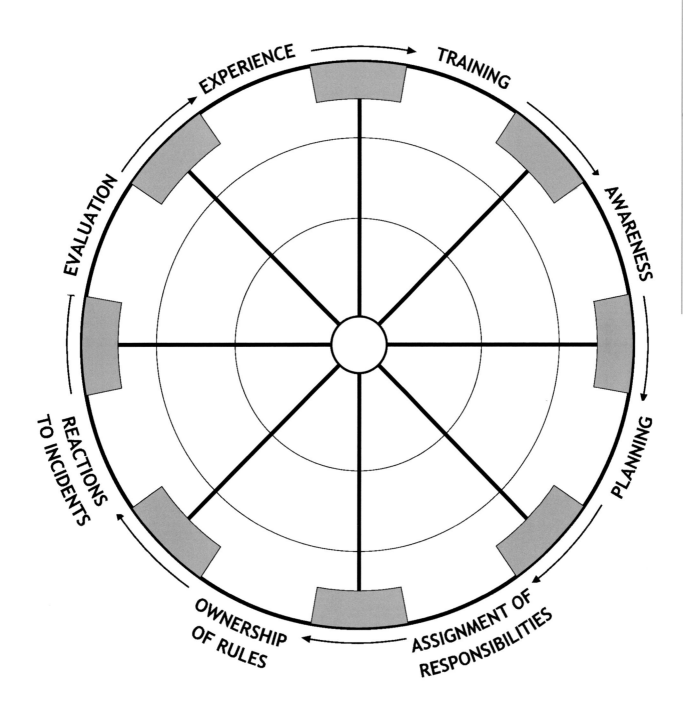

The security wheel is never perfect:

Some of its parts are more developed than others. It is therefore more useful to examine the degree of development of each part. This way, you can identify which types of action you should prioritize to improve your protection and security. Each thin line going from the center outwards illustrates how developed this component of the wheel is.

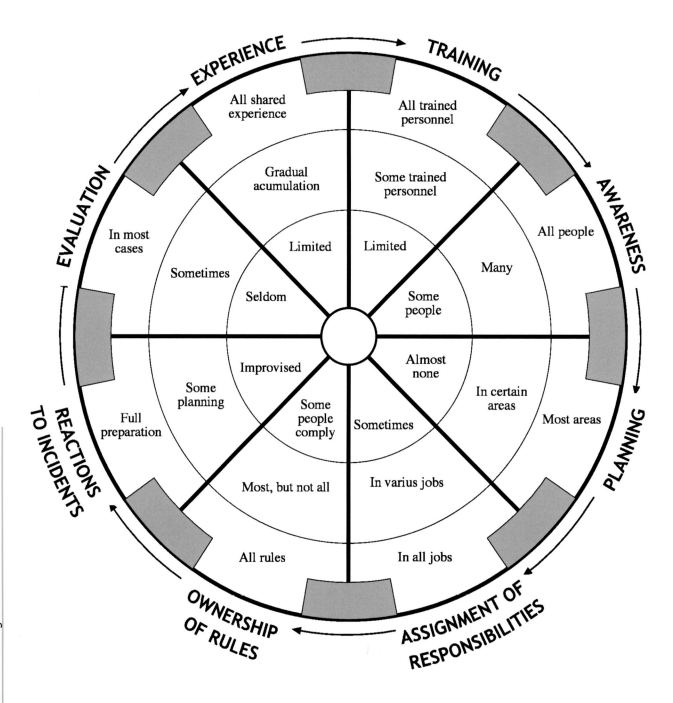

Photocopy the wheel on paper or acetate and add color to the spaces between the spokes. This will illustrate the real shape of your group's or organization's wheel, and make it easier to see which parts are more - and less - developed.

If any of the wheel's eight components fail, you will have to determine:

 What the problems are with this part of the wheel…

…and what the solutions to these problems are.

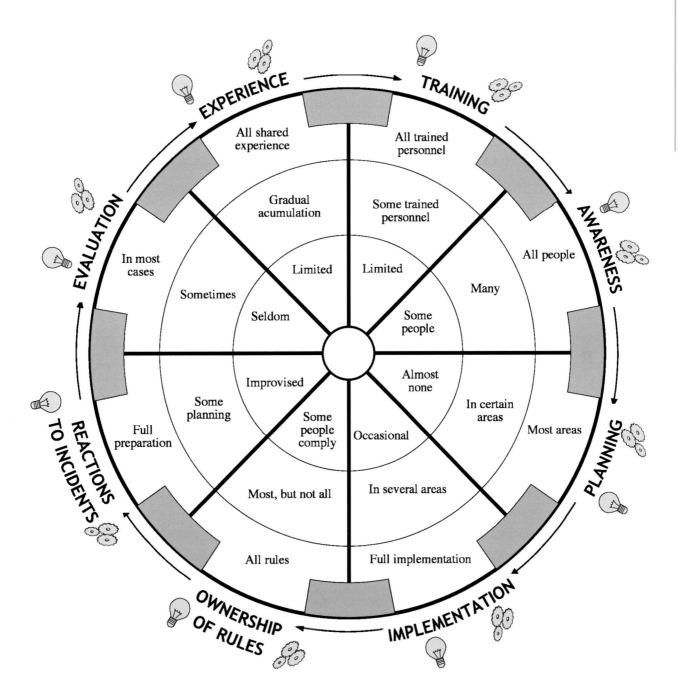

CHAPTER   8

Making sure security rules and procedures are followed

Purpose

Thinking about what makes staff and organisations unable or unwilling to follow security plans and procedures, and finding appropriate solutions.

Security is everybody's business

The issue of whether people and organisations actually follow security procedures and rules is a complex one. It is perfectly possible to have a good security plan, complete with preventive rules and emergency procedures; you can place security high on the agenda at all big meetings, etc, but people may still not follow the organisation's security rules.

This could seem incredible, given that human rights defenders are constantly under pressure and being threatened. But it happens.

If someone wants to know something about your work, they will not try to find out from the most careful person in the organisation. Rather, they will try to get close to someone who often gets drunk on Saturday nights. Similarly, if someone wants to give your organisation a fright, they probably will not assault a person who has taken all the necessary precautions. Rather, they will probably target someone who is usually quite careless about their own security. Similarly, it could be that a careful person is attacked because the careless person left the door open... The point is also that one person's carelessness can place everyone at greater risk.

This is why security should be defined as an issue for the whole organisation, in addition to the individuals it involves. If only three out of 12 people follow the security rules, the whole organisation, including those who observe the rules, is put at risk. If the situation improves and nine people start following security procedures, the risk is reduced. But the risk would still be much smaller if all 12 people followed the rules.

Security is an issue
for the whole organisation,
as well as for
the individuals it involves.

Having a good security plan is meaningless unless it is being followed. Let's be realistic: Many people do not follow the rules or procedures. This lack of compliance amounts to the difference between good intentions and real-life effectiveness. It is nevertheless easier to confront this problem than its possible consequences.

Why don't people follow security rules, and how can we avoid this from the outset?

First of all, the word "compliance" carries connotations of submissiveness and docility and should therefore be avoided. People only follow rules which they understand and accept, because they can then make them their own. The key word here is therefore "ownership".

In order for a security procedure to be followed, everyone in the organisation has to embrace it. This doesn't happen instantly. In order for staff to embrace a security procedure they must be allowed to participate in drawing it up and implementing it. Training, understanding and acceptance of the procedure are also crucial.

Table 1: The relationship between individuals and organisations in security terms

CONCEPT	APPROACH: "EVERYONE MUST FOLLOW THE RULES!"	APPROACH: "THE INDIVIDUAL AND THE ORGANISATION HAVE AGREED ON THE RULES!"
APPROACH	Rule-focused	Based on organisational and personal security needs
TYPE OF RELATIONSHIP BETWEEN THE INDIVIDUAL AND THE ORGANISATION	Normative or "paternalistic"	Based on dialogue
WHY DO WE FOLLOW THE RULES?	By obligation, to avoid sanction or expulsion	To observe an agreement, with room for criticism and improvement (because we agree with the purpose/need, in order to help protect our colleagues and the people we work with/for)
RESPONSIBILITY FOR SECURITY	Not shared	Shared

Ownership is not just about "following rules", but about establishing an agreement about the rules that will make individuals follow them because they understand them, see them as appropriate and effective, and feel they have a personal stake in them. For this reason, the rules should also conform to individuals' moral and ethical criteria and basic needs.

Ownership is not about simply "following rules",
but about respecting an agreement between the organisation
and staff regarding security.

In order to maintain the agreement between staff members and the organisation it is important that **the individual(s) responsible for security keep others constantly involved** through briefings, reminders about aspects of the agreement, and by asking for people's opinions on how appropriate and effective the rules are in practice.

Such involvement will however be of little value without an **organisational culture of security** which underpins formal and informal work procedures or programmes.

The necessary basis for people to observe security rules and procedures can be achieved through the following steps:

◆ Developing an understanding that security is important for the protection of victims, witnesses, family members and colleagues, to enable the core work of the organization to continue.

◆ Developing and valuing an organisational security culture.

◆ Creating ownership of security rules and procedures.

◆ Making sure all staff participate in designing and improving security rules and procedures.

◆ Training people in security issues.

◆ Making sure all staff are convinced about the appropriateness and effectiveness of security rules and procedures.

◆ Establishing an agreement between the organisation and individuals about respecting security rules and procedures.

◆ Involving those responsible for security in briefing and training people; in reminding staff of the terms of the agreement and asking their opinions on how appropriate and effective the rules are in practice.

Why security rules and procedures are not followed

There is no prototype of a human rights defender who doesn't follow security rules. Many people within an organisation often follow some rules but not others, or observe the rules sporadically.

There are many possible reasons why people don't observe the rules and procedures. To change this and ensure ownership, it is important to establish the causes and find solutions alongside the other people concerned. It will also be useful to distinguish between the different reasons people may have to not follow the rules, because they will vary.

Some possible reasons for not observing security rules and procedures:

Unintentional:

- The defender is unaware of the rules.
- S/he doesn't apply the rules properly.

Intentional:

General problems:

- The rules are too complicated and difficult to follow.
- The procedures aren't within easy reach in the office or are presented in a way that makes them difficult to use day-to-day.

Individual problems:

- The rules are at odds with the individual's needs or interests and this conflict hasn't been resolved.
- The individual does not agree with some or all of the rules and considers them unnecessary, inappropriate or ineffective based on personal experience, previous information or training or because of personal beliefs.

Group problems:

- Most staff don't follow the rules, or group 'leaders' either don't follow them or don't do so enough, because there is no organisational security culture.
- A general lack of motivation at work can lead people to ignore security rules.

Organisational problems:

- There aren't sufficient financial or technical resources to make it easy for staff to follow the rules.
- There's a contradiction between the rules and particular areas of work. For example, rules have been established by those in charge of security but ignored or not properly implemented by people working in programmes or accounts. Some rules might suit one work area and contradict another.
- Staff have a heavy workload and limited time, and don't prioritise some or all of the rules.
- A general lack of motivation, arising as a result of stress, workplace disputes, etc.

Organisational culture is both formal and informal, and must be developed not just in the organisation as a whole, but also in teams. A good organisational culture will show signs such as informal chatting, joking, parties, etc.

Monitoring the observance of security rules and procedures

Direct monitoring:

Security rules and procedures can be incorporated in general work appraisals and "check-lists"; as well as in meetings before and after field missions, in work reports, on meeting agendas, etc.

Periodical reviews can also be carried out together with the teams in question, of issues such as the safe-keeping of sensitive information, copies and security manuals; of security protocols for visits to the organisation's headquarters; preparing to go on field missions, and so on.

Indirect monitoring:

Asking people for their views about rules and procedures, whether they are appropriate and easy to follow, etc, can establish whether staff actually know about the rules, whether they have been fully accepted or if there is disagreement which should be dealt with. Staff use of the security manual and any existing protocols and rules can also be reviewed.

It is very worthwhile to compile and analyse along with the people or teams in question, people's opinions and evaluations of security rules and procedures. This can also be done off the record/anonymously or via a third party.

Retrospective monitoring:

Security can be reviewed by analysing security incidents as they arise. This must be handled especially carefully. Someone who has experienced a security incident might worry that it was their fault and/or that analysis will lead to sanctions against them. S/he might therefore be tempted to conceal it, leaving the incident, or aspects of it, unreported.

Who does the monitoring?

Depending on the way the organisation operates, whoever is responsible for organising security, specific areas of work within security, and managing any security staff, will also be in charge of monitoring security.

What can we do if security rules and procedures aren't being followed?

1 ◆ Establish the causes, find solutions and put them into practice. The list of options in Table 1 above can be used as a guide.

2 ◆ If the problem is intentional and only involves one individual, try to

    a ◆ engage in a dialogue with the person to establish the cause(s) or motive.

    b ◆ work with the individual's whole team (this can sometimes be inappropriate, depending on the case).

c ◆ apply a notice or warning system, so that the person is fully aware of the problem.

d ◆ use a system of gradual sanctions which could culminate in the person being sacked.

3 ◆ Include a clause about observing security rules and procedures in all work contracts, in order for all staff to be fully aware of how important this is to the organisation.

In conclusion,

Some may argue that a discussion of the reasons why people don't follow security rules is a waste of time, as there are more urgent or important things to be done. Those of that opinion normally think simply that rules are to be followed, full stop. Others are aware that the world doesn't always work that way.

Whatever your opinion, we now invite you to step back and analyse the degree to which security rules and procedures are being followed in the organisation(s) where you work. The results could be surprising and worth spending time on in order to avoid problems further down the line...

Improving security at work and at home

Purpose

Assess security at work or at home.

Planning, improving and checking security in offices and homes.

Security at work and at home

Security at the organisation's headquarters or offices and in staff members' homes is of fundamental importance to human rights defenders' work. We will therefore go into some depth about how the security of an office or home can be analysed and improved. *(For the sake of simplicity we will just refer to "offices" from now on, although the information below also applies to home security.)*

General aspects of office security

Our aims in improving security can be summarised in three words: **Prevent unauthorised access**. In rare cases it is also necessary to protect an office against a possible attack (against bombing, for example).

This brings us to the first general consideration - the vulnerabilities of an office. These serve to increase risk, depending on the threat you are facing. For example, if you are at risk of someone stealing equipment or information, you must remove your vulnerabilities accordingly. A night alarm is of little use if nobody is going to come and check what has happened. On the other hand, if there is a violent break-in in daylight, reinforced railings on the door or alarms won't be very useful. In short, take measures according to the threats you face and the context you are working in.

> The vulnerabilities
> of an office
> must be assessed
> in the light of
> the threats you may face.

However, it is important to find a balance between putting appropriate security measures in place and giving outsiders the impression that something is being "hidden" or "guarded", because this can in itself put you at risk. In office security you often have to choose between keeping a low profile or taking more obvious measures if need be.

> The security
> of an office
> is no greater than
> its weakest point.

If somebody wants to gain entry without your knowledge, they won't choose the most difficult point of entry to do it. Remember that the easiest way of gaining access to an office and observing what goes on inside is sometimes simply to knock on the door and go inside.

The office location

Factors to consider when setting up an office are: The neighbourhood; whether the building is associated with any particular people or activities from the past; accessibility on public and private transport; risk of accidents; how suitable the building is for putting the necessary security measures in place, etc. (Also see *Location evaluation risk* below.)

It is useful to review which security measures are being taken by others in the neighbourhood. If there are many, this may be a sign of an unsafe area, for example, in respect of common crime. It is also important to talk to people in the area about the local security situation. In any case, make sure security measures can be taken without attracting undue attention. It is also useful to get to know local people as they can pass on information regarding anything suspicious going on in the neighbourhood.

It is also important to check out who is your landlord. How is their reputation? Could they be susceptible to pressure from the authorities? Will they be comfortable with you putting security measures in place?

The choice of office must take account of who needs to come to the office. An office where victims come to seek legal advice will have different requirements to an office which is primarily a place for staff to work. It is important to take account of how easy it is to get to by public transport, will it result in unsafe journeys between the area where staff live, those where most work activities take place, etc. The surrounding areas must be evaluated, especially in order to avoid having to travel through unsafe areas.

Once the location has been selected, it is important to do periodical evaluations of aspects of the location which can vary, for example, if an 'undesirable element' moves into the neighbourhood.

CHECKLIST FOR CHOOSING A GOOD OFFICE LOCATION	
NEIGHBOURHOOD:	Crime statistics; closeness to potential targets of armed attacks, such as military or government installations; secure locations for taking refuge; other national or international organisations with whom you have a relationship.
RELATIONSHIPS:	Type of people in the neighbourhood; owner/landlord, former tenants; former uses of the building.
ACCESSIBILITY:	One or several good access routes (the more, the better); accessibility by public and private transport.
BASIC SERVICES:	Water and electricity, phone.
STREET LIGHTING	In the surrounding area.
SUSCEPTIBILITY TO ACCIDENTS OR NATURAL RISKS:	Fires, serious flooding, landslides, dumping of dangerous materials, factories with hazardous industrial processes, etc.
PHYSICAL STRUCTURE:	Solidity of structures, facility for installing security equipment, doors and windows, perimeter and protection barriers, access points (see below).
FOR VEHICLES:	A garage or at least a courtyard or enclosed space, with a parking barrier.

Third-party access to the office: Physical barriers and visitor procedures

You now know that the primary purpose of office security is denying unauthorised people access. One or several people could enter to steal, acquire information, plant something which can later be used against you, such as drugs or weapons, threaten you, etc. Every case is different, but the aim remains the same: Avoid it.

Access to a building is controlled through **physical barriers** (fences, doors, gates), through **technical measures** (such as alarms with lighting) and **visitor admission procedures**. Every barrier and procedure is a **filter** through which anyone who wishes to gain access to the office must pass. Ideally, these filters should be combined to form several layers of protection, capable of preventing different types of unauthorised entry.

Barriers serve to **physically** block the entry of unauthorised visitors. How useful physical barriers are depends on their **solidity** and ability to cover **all vulnerable gaps** in the walls.

Your office can have physical barriers in three areas:

1 ◆ The **external** perimeter: Fences, walls or similar, beyond a garden or courtyard.

2 ◆ The perimeter of the **building or premises**.

3 ◆ The **internal** perimeter: Barriers which can be created within an office to protect one or several rooms. This is particularly useful in offices with many visitors passing through, as it allows for a separate public area and a more private one which can be protected with additional barriers.

The external perimeter

The office should be surrounded by a clear external perimeter, possibly with high or low fences, preferably solid and high to make access more difficult. Railings or see-through wire mesh will make the organisation's work more visible, and it is therefore better to have brick walls or similar.

The perimeter of the building or premises

This includes walls, doors, windows and ceiling or roof. If the walls are solid, all the openings and the roof will also be solid. Doors and windows must have adequate locks and be reinforced with grills, preferably with both horizontal and vertical bars well embedded into the wall. If there is a roof, it should offer good protection - not just a simple sheet of zinc or a layer of tiles. If the roof cannot be reinforced, block all possible access to the roof from the ground or neighbouring buildings.

In a location with a risk of armed attack, it is important to establish secure areas within the office (see Chapter 11 on security in areas of armed conflict).

The internal perimeter

The same applies here as to the building or premises. It is very useful to have an area with additional security inside the office, and this is usually very easy to arrange. Even a safety deposit box can be considered an internal security perimeter.

A note on keys

☐ No keys should be visible or accessible to visitors. Keep all keys in a cupboard or drawer with a simple combination lock which only staff know the code to. Make sure that the code is changed from time to time for greater security.

☐ If keys are individually labelled, do not mark them with a description of the corresponding room, cupboard or drawer, as this will make a robbery much easier. Use number, letter or colour coding instead.

Technical measures strengthen physical barriers or procedures for admitting visitors, such as spy holes, intercoms and video cameras (see below). This is because **technical measures are only useful when they are activated to deter intruders**. In order to work, a technical measure must provoke a particular reaction, for example, attracting attention from neighbours, the police or a private security firm. If this does not happen, and the intruder knows that it won't, such measures are of little use and will be reduced to preventing petty theft or recording the people who enter.

☐ **Lighting** around the building (of courtyards, gardens, pavement) and on landings is essential.

☐ **Alarms** have several purposes, including detecting intruders and deterring potential intruders from entering or from continuing to attempt access.

An alarm can activate a warning sound inside the office; a security light; a general, loud tone, bell or noise; or a signal in an external security centre. An audio alarm is useful for attracting attention but can be counter-productive in conflict situations or if you don't expect local residents or others to react to it. A careful choice must be made between an audio and light alarm (a fixed powerful light, and an intermittent red light). The latter can be enough to deter an intruder, because it suggests that something else will happen following initial detection.

Alarms should be installed at access points (courtyards, doors and windows, and vulnerable premises such as rooms containing sensitive information). The most straightforward alarms are **motion** sensors, which activate a light, emit a noise or activate a camera when they detect movement.

Alarms should:

◆ have a **battery**, so it can function during power cuts.

◆ have a **delay** before it activates so it can be deactivated by staff who might set it off accidentally.

◆ include an option for **manual** activation in case staff need to turn it on.

◆ be easy to **install** and **maintain**.

◆ be easily **distinguishable** from a fire alarm.

Video cameras

Video cameras can help improve admission procedures (see below) or record people who enter the office. However, the recording must be made from a point which is beyond the reach of an intruder. Otherwise intruders can break open the camera and destroy the tape.

You may need to consider whether cameras will intimidate people you want to come and visit you such as victims or witnesses, or whether they will be seen as a valuable commodity which will attract thieves. It is good practice to post a warning notice if you are using a camera (the right to privacy is also a human right).

Private security companies

This area requires great care. In many countries, private security firms are staffed by ex-security force members. There are documented cases of such people being involved in surveillance of, and attacks on, human rights defenders. It therefore makes sense not to trust security companies if you have reason to fear surveillance or attacks by security forces. If a security company has access to your offices, they could plant microphones or allow other people in.

If you feel you need to use a security company you should ensure that you have a clear agreement about what their personnel are allowed to do, and not allowed to do on your behalf, and which parts of the building they can access. Of course, you also must be able to monitor that these agreements are fulfilled.

For example:

If you have hired a security service that sends a guard in case an alarm break off, this guard may have access to sensitive parts of your office and might set up listening devices in your meeting room.

It is better if you can agree (and if possible screen) which specific staff will be working for you, but this is rarely possible.

If the security guards carry weapons it is important for a human rights organization to have a clear understanding about what their rules are for using them. But it is even more important to outweigh the potential benefits of using weapons against their drawbacks. Small arms are not a deterrence against attackers with higher fire capacity (as it is usually the case), but if attackers know that there are carriers of short guns within your premises, the may decide to break in ready to open fire, to protect themselves during the attack. In other words, some armed capacity (small arms) will probably lead attackers to open use of arms with higher fire capacity. At this point it is worth asking yourself, if you need guards with sub-machine guns, do you have the minimum socio-political space in which to carry out your work?

Admission procedure filters

Physical barriers must be accompanied by an **admission procedure** "filter". Such procedures determine when, how and who gains access to any part of the office. Access to sensitive areas, such as keys, information and money, must be restricted.

The easiest way to gain entry to an office where human rights defenders work is to knock on the door and go inside. Many people do this every day. In order to reconcile the open character of a human rights office with the need to control who wants to visit you and why, you need appropriate admission procedures.

In general, people have a particular reason to want to enter or knock on your door. They often want to ask a question or to deliver something, without necessarily asking permission first. Let's examine this case by case:

Someone calls and asks for permission to enter for a particular reason

You should then follow three simple steps:

1 ◆ **Ask why the person wishes to enter.** If s/he wants to see somebody in the office, consult the latter. If that person is not present, ask the visitor to return at another time or to wait somewhere outside the restricted office area. It is important to use spyholes, cameras or entry phones to avoid having to open or approach a door, especially if you want to refuse someone entry or are facing violent or forced entry. It is therefore good to have a waiting area which is physically separate from the office's internal entrance. If an easily accessible public area is essential, ensure that there are physical barriers blocking access to restricted parts of the office.

Someone could request entry in order to check or repair the water or electricity supply or carry out other maintenance work. S/he could also claim to be a media representative, a state official, etc. Always confirm their identity with the company or organisation they claim to be representing before allowing them entry. Remember that neither a uniform nor an identity card are guarantees of proper and secure identification, especially in a medium or high risk situation.

2 ◆ **Decide whether or not to allow access.** Once your visitor's reason for entering has been established, you'll need to decide whether or not to allow them in. Just because someone states a reason for entering isn't a good enough reason to let them in. If you are not sure what their errand is, don't allow access.

3 ◆ **Supervise visitors until they leave.** Once a visitor has entered the office, make sure that someone is supervising them at all times until they leave. It is useful to have a separate area to meet with visitors, away from the restricted areas.

A record should be kept of every visitor with name, organization, purpose of visit, who they met with, when arrived, when left. This can be particularly useful when reviewing what went wrong after a security incident.

Someone arrives or calls asking questions

Regardless of what a caller or visitor might say, you should under no circumstances tell them the location of a colleague or other people nearby, nor give them any personal information. If s/he is insistent, offer to leave a message, ask them to come or call back later or make an appointment with the person they wish to see.

People can often show up mistakenly, asking if so-and-so lives there or if something is for sale, etc. Some also want to sell things, and beggars can come looking for help. If you deny these people access and information, you will avoid any security risk.

Someone wants to deliver an object or package

The risk you run with a package or object is that the contents could compromise or hurt you, especially in case of a package or letter bomb. No matter how innocent it may look, do not touch or handle a package until you have taken these three simple steps:

1 ◆ **Check if the intended recipient is expecting the package.** It is not enough that the recipient knows the sender, because the sender's identity could easily be faked. If the intended recipient is not expecting a package, s/he must check that the supposed sender has actually sent them something. If the package is simply addressed to your office, check who sent it. Wait and discuss the issue before making a final decision.

2 ◆ **Decide whether or not to accept the package or letter.** If you can't establish who sent the package, or if this will take time, the best option is not to accept it, especially in a medium or high risk environment. You can always ask for it to be delivered later, or collect it at the post office.

3 ◆ **Keep track of the package inside the office.** Make sure you know where in the office the package is, at all times until the recipient accepts it.

During functions or parties

In these circumstances, the rule is simple: Do not let anyone whom you don't know first hand enter. Only people who are known to trusted colleagues should enter, and only when that colleague is present and can identify their guest. If a person shows up saying they know someone in the office who isn't there, don't let them in.

Keeping records of phone calls and visitors

It may also be useful to keep a record of phone calls and phone numbers and – keeping record of people that visit the organization (in some organizations, new visitors are requested to present an identity document and the organization registers the number of the document)

Working extra-hours at the office

There should be procedures for staff working extra-hours. Members of an organization intending to work extra-hours late at night should report by certain hours with another designated member, take special care when leaving the premises, etc.

CHECKLIST: IDENTIFYING WEAK POINTS IN ADMISSION PROCEDURES
◆ **Who** has regular access to **which** areas and **why**? Restrict access unless it is absolutely necessary.
◆ Distinguish between different **types** of visitors (messengers, maintenance workers, computer technicians, NGO members for meetings, VIPs, guests for functions, etc,) and **develop appropriate admission procedures for each**. All staff should be familiar with all procedures for all types of visitors, and take responsibility for carrying them out.
◆ Once a visitor enters the office, can they access weak points? Develop strategies to prevent this.
CHECKLIST: ACCESS TO KEYS
◆ **Who** has access to **which** keys and **when**?
◆ Where and how are **keys** and **copies** of those **kept**?
◆ Is there a record of key copies that are in circulation?
◆ Is there a risk that somebody will make an **unauthorised key copy**?
◆ What happens **if somebody loses a key**? The corresponding lock must be changed, unless you are absolutely sure that it has been accidentally mislaid and that nobody can identify the owner of the key or your address. Remember that a key can be stolen – for example, in a staged robbery – in order for someone to gain access to the office.

All staff members have a responsibility to take action against anyone who is not properly observing the admission procedures. They should also make a note in the security incidents book of any movements by suspicious people or vehicles. The same applies to any object placed outside the building, in order to rule out the potential risk of a bomb. If you suspect a bomb, don't ignore it, **don't touch it**, and do contact the police.

When moving offices, or if keys have been lost or stolen, it is essential to change all the locks in the entrance area, at the very least.

Checklist: General office security procedures

☐ Provide fire extinguishers and flashlights (with replaceable batteries). Make sure all staff members know how to use them.

☐ Provide an electricity generator if there is a strong possibility of power cuts. Power cuts can endanger security (lights, alarms, telephones, etc.), particularly in rural areas.

□ Keep a list handy of local emergency numbers for police, fire brigade, ambulance, nearby hospitals for emergencies, etc.

□ If there is a risk of conflict nearby, keep a supply of food and water in reserve.

□ Establish the location of secure areas outside the office for emergencies (for example, the offices of other organisations).

□ Nobody from outside the organisation must be left **alone** in a vulnerable area with access to keys, information or valuables.

□ **Keys:** Never leave keys where visitors might have access to them. Never "hide" keys outside the office entrance – this makes them accessible, not hidden.

□ **Admission procedures:** Security barriers offer no protection if a potential intruder is allowed to enter the office. The main points to bear in mind are:

 ◆ All staff are equally responsible for visitor control and admission.

 ◆ All visitors must be accompanied at all times while in the office.

□ If an unauthorised visitor is found in the office:

 ◆ Never confront someone who seems prepared to use violence to get what they want (for example, if they are armed). In such cases, alert colleagues, find a safe place to hide and try to get help from the police.

 ◆ Approach the person carefully or seek assistance in the office or from the police.

□ In high risk situations, always keep control of vulnerable things, such as the information stored on a hard drive, in order to make them inaccessible or remove them in case of an emergency evacuation.

□ Bear in mind that in case of confrontation with a potential intruder, the people working in the office are on the front line. Ensure that they have the necessary training and support at all times to deal with any situation, and without putting themselves at risk.

Regular inspections of office security

Regular supervision or inspection of office security is very important, because security situations and procedures vary over time, for example, because equipment deteriorates or if there is a high staff turnover. It is also important to achieve some sense of staff ownership of the office security rules.

The person responsible for security must carry out at least one review of office security **every six months**. With the help of the list below this can take as little as one or two hours. The person in charge of security must ensure that staff feedback is sought before the final report is written, and then present the security report to the organisation in order for the necessary decisions to be made and for action to be taken. The report should then be kept on file until the next security review.

CHECKLIST: OFFICE SECURITY REVIEW

REVIEW OF:
CARRIED OUT BY:
DATE:

1 ◆ EMERGENCY CONTACTS:

◆ Is there a handy and up to date list with telephone numbers and addresses of other local NGOs, emergency hospitals, police, fire brigade and ambulance?

2 ◆ TECHNICAL AND PHYSICAL BARRIERS (EXTERNAL, INTERNAL AND INTERIOR):

◆ Check condition and working order of external gates/fences, doors to the building, windows, walls and roof.

◆ Check condition and working order of external lighting, alarms, cameras or video entrance phones.

◆ Check key procedures, including that keys are kept securely and code-labelled, assignment of responsibility for controlling keys and copies, and that keys and copies are in good working order. Make sure locks are changed when keys are lost or stolen, and that such incidents are logged.

3 ◆ VISITOR ADMISSION PROCEDURES AND "FILTERS":

◆ Are admission procedures in operation for all types of visitors? Are all staff familiar with them?

◆ Review all recorded security incidents related to admission procedures or "filters".

◆ Ask those staff members who usually carry out admission procedures if the procedures are working properly, and what improvements are needed.

4 ◆ SECURITY IN CASE OF ACCIDENTS:

◆ Check the condition of fire extinguishers, gas valves/pipes and water taps, electricity plugs and cables and electricity generators (where applicable).

5 ◆ RESPONSIBILITY AND TRAINING:

◆ Has responsibility for office security been assigned? Is it effective?

◆ Is there an office security training programme? Does it cover all the areas included in this review? Have all new staff members been trained? Is the training effective?

Security and women human rights defenders

Purpose

Looking at the specific security needs of women human rights defenders.

The following attempts to cover some basic points about the specific needs of women human rights defenders. This is a topic which requires more in-depth analysis based on the practical experiences of women human rights defenders. It is intended that more detailed materials on this topic will be produced in the context of the International Consultation on Women Human Rights defenders in 2005.

Women as defenders of human rights

Women have always been important actors in the promotion and protection of human rights however, their role has not always been positively acknowledged. Women work on their own and alongside men in the defence of human rights[1]. Many women belong to organisations working on behalf of disappeared people and prisoners. Others defend the rights of minority groups or victims of sexual violence, and others are trade unionists, lawyers and campaigners for land rights.

Attacks on women human rights defenders

In her **2002 annual report to the Commission on Human Rights** Hina Jilani, UN Secretary General's Special Representative on Human Rights Defenders states:

> Women human rights defenders are on a par with their male colleagues in putting themselves on the front line in the promotion and protection of human rights. In doing so, however, as women, they face risks that are specific to their gender and additional to those faced by men.

[1] A very useful guide on women human rights defenders UNHCHR website at http://www.unhchr.ch/defenders/tiwomen.htm. Also see *Report: Consultation on Women HRDs with the UN Special Representative of the Secretary General on Human Rights Defenders, April 4-6 2003*, Published by Asia Pacific Forum on Women, Law and Development, and *Essential actors of our time. Human rights defenders in the Americas*, by Amnesty International.

In the first instance, as women, they become more visible. That is, women defenders may arouse more hostility than their male colleagues because as women human rights defenders they may defy cultural, religious or social norms about femininity and the role of women in a particular country or society. In this context, not only may they face human rights violations for their work as human rights defenders, but even more so because of their gender and the fact that their work may run counter to societal stereotypes about women's submissive nature, or challenge notions of the society about the status of women.

Secondly, it is not unlikely that the hostility, harassment and repression women defenders face may themselves take a gender specific form, ranging from, for example, verbal abuse directed exclusively at women because of their gender to sexual harassment and rape.

In this connection, women's professional integrity and standing in society can be threatened and discredited in ways that are specific to them, such as the all too familiar pretextual calling into question of their probity when - for example - women assert their right to sexual and reproductive health, or to equality with men, including to a life free from discrimination and violence. In this context, for example, women human rights defenders have been tried using laws criminalizing conduct amounting to the legitimate enjoyment and exercise of rights protected under international law on spurious charges brought against them simply because of their views and advocacy work in defence of women's rights.

Thirdly, human rights abuses perpetrated against women human rights defenders can, in turn, have repercussions that are, in and of themselves, gender-specific. For example, the sexual abuse of a woman human rights defender in custody and her rape can result in pregnancy and sexually transmitted diseases, including HIV/AIDS.

Certain women-specific rights are almost exclusively promoted and protected by women human rights defenders. Promoting and protecting women's rights can be an additional risk factor, as the assertion of some such rights is seen as a threat to patriarchy and as disruptive of cultural, religious and societal mores. Defending women's right to life and liberty in some countries has resulted in the life and liberty of women defenders themselves being violated. Similarly, protesting against discriminatory practices has led to the prosecution of a prominent women's rights defender on charges of apostasy.

Factors such as age, ethnicity, educational background, sexual orientation and marital status must also be taken into consideration, as different groups of women defenders face different challenges and therefore have different protection and security needs.

The assessment of protection needs of women defenders will help to clarify the specific and often different needs, vulnerabilities and coping strategies of women defenders. This way, their situations can be more adequately addressed in emergency and day to day situations.

Security for women human rights defenders

Women human rights defenders are paying a heavy price for their work in protecting and promoting other people's human rights. Women defenders have to confront risks which are specific to their gender, and their security therefore requires a specific approach. Here's a list of causes for this:

Women may attract unwanted attention.

Women defenders may provoke hostility because being both a woman and a human rights defender could defy local cultural, religious or social norms about femininity and women's role. Women defenders could therefore face human rights violations not just because of their work, but simply because being a working woman, or a defender, can challenge a society's stereotypes about women's submissive nature and ideas about their status.

Women defenders may have to break patriarchal laws and social taboos.

In some countries, defending women's right to life and liberty has resulted in the life and liberty of women defenders themselves being violated. Similarly, protesting against discriminatory practices has led to a prominent women's rights defender being prosecuted on charges of apostasy. In many cultures, the requirement that women should defer to men in public can be an obstacle to women publicly questioning human rights violations carried out by men. Certain discriminatory or sexist interpretations of religious texts are also often used to maintain or establish laws or practices which have a major influence on women's rights.

There are specific forms of attack against women defenders.

The hostility, harassment and repression women defenders face may be gender-specific, ranging from verbal abuse directed exclusively at them to sexual harassment and rape. The consequences of such attacks can also be gender-specific, such as pregnancy and social rejection.

Women defenders may come under pressure to "prove" their integrity:

Women's professionalism and standing in society can be threatened and discredited in ways that are specific to them, such as their integrity being called into question.

Male colleagues may not understand, or could even reject, women defenders' work:

Male colleagues of women human rights defenders can have the same social prejudices as outsiders who attack women defenders. Men could also feel threatened by professional competition from a woman. This can result in attempts to marginalise or undermine women human rights defenders and can sometimes result in harassment and violence against women defenders by their colleagues.

Domestic violence can result from changing power structures within a family. A woman defender's growing professional role and empowerment could make her husband, partner or other family members feel threatened and lead him/her to try to stop her activities or become violent. Domestic violence against women includes all physical, sexual and psychological harm which occurs within the family, such as battering, marital rape, female genital mutilation and other traditional practices which are harmful to women (see below).

Additional family obligations:

Many women defenders have to take care of children and other relatives, in addition to their other work. Such responsibilities, especially if involving young children, will influence many of the security decisions a woman defender may have to make in a high risk situation.

Moving towards better security and protection for women human rights defenders

It is important to recognise that women defenders constitute a wide range of individuals who face different problems, have different backgrounds and require different solutions. The most important point to remember is that, in any given security situation, women are human rights defenders who can identify problems and find appropriate solutions. In order to do this, a combination of mainstreaming women's participation, ensuring gender specific security issues are addressed and providing training is necessary:

Mainstreaming women's participation

In a nutshell, this means ensuring full participation by women alongside men in decision-making; putting women's security issues on the agenda, and placing women on a par with men in the process of taking security precautions. It is important to include women's experiences and perceptions and to ensure that women are defining security rules and procedures, as well as monitoring and evaluating them.

Ensuring gender specific security and protection needs are addressed

As with other security needs, assigning responsibilities for addressing gender-based violence and security risks of women defenders is very important within any defender organisation or group. Ideally the individuals responsible for security will have a good understanding of the specific needs of women defenders. It may sometimes be necessary to identify someone else who can bring in specific knowledge and understanding to the issue. For example, one person might be in charge of security, but the organisation later decides to appoint a person with the training and skills to be a focal point for gender-based violence. In such cases, both people must work closely together to ensure that all security procedures run smoothly and respond to people's different needs.

Training

Training for all those working together in a human rights organization is key to improving security and protection and should include developing awareness about the specific needs of women defenders.

Gender-based violence is always **underreported**. A general awareness about gender-based violence within the organisation or group can make it easier for people to talk about gender specific threats or incidents. Willing staff members can also serve as "entry-points" for women and men defenders who want to find solutions to gender-based threats or violence against them or others in the organisation or community.

In summary,

Differences in women's security needs are linked to their different roles, to different kinds of threats, and to differences between specific situations (such as detention, field work, etc.) The aim is to develop gender-sensitive responses to violence against women and other defenders.

Sexual assaults and personal security

The prevention of a sexual assault can be similar to that of other attacks, especially those associated with common crime. Sexual assaults can take the form of repression of defenders' work, and victims can either be pre-selected or opportunistic targets.

Everyone - male and female - is a potential victim of sexual assault, but women are more frequent targets. Sexual assault is a crime of **power** and violence, and sexual contact is just another way for the attacker to demonstrate his or her power over the victim.

Remember that in many cases women taken to a different location with a potential attacker are raped (and beaten or even killed): Thus women should always make a strong and definite decision not to go with a potential attacker to another location (probably unless such a refusal would severely endanger her life or the life of others).

Reacting to a sexual assault[2]

The options for response to a sexual assault are limited and strictly up to the victim. There is no right or wrong way to react. In all cases, the primary objective is to survive. The options available to the victim of a sexual assault can include doing the following:

1 ◆ Submit. If the victim fears for his or her life, they may choose to submit to the crime.

2 ◆ Passive resistance. Do or say anything distasteful or disgusting to ruin the attacker's desire for sexual contact. Tell him you have AIDS, diarrhea, make yourself vomit, etc.

3 ◆ Active resistance: Try any type of physical force you can muster to fight off the attacker, such as striking, kicking, biting, scratching, shouting and running away.

In all cases, do whatever you must to survive. Go with your instincts. No one knows how they will react in such a situation and your way to react will be right for you and the given situation.

After a sexual assault

All human rights defender organisations and groups should have preventive and reactive plans in place to deal with sexual assaults. The reactive plan should include, at the very least, providing the victim with **effective healthcare, including psychological care, (**check immediately and regularly for sexually-transmitted diseases, day-after pill, etc) **and legal care.**

A careful balance must be struck between ensuring the victim has access to the relevant specialist support and ensuring the organization reacts in an appropriately supportive way.

Please also see *Preventing and reacting to attacks* in Chapter 5.

---

[2] Most of this information has been adapted from Van Brabant's book *Operational Security in Violent Environments* and from World Vision's and the World Council of Churches' Security Manuals.

THE DECLARATION ON THE ELIMINATION OF VIOLENCE
AGAINST WOMEN (1993) DEFINES VIOLENCE AGAINST
WOMEN AS:

Any act of gender-based violence that results in, or is likely to result in, physical, sexual or psychological harm or suffering to women, including threats of such acts, coercion orarbitrary deprivation of liberty, whether occurring in public or in private life. (Article 1)

Violence against women shall be understood to encompass, but not be limited to, thefollowing:

a) ◆ Physical, sexual and psychological violence occurring in the family, including battering, sexual abuse of female children in the household, dowry-related violence, marital rape, female genital mutilation and other traditional practices harmful to women, non-spousal violence and violence related to exploitation.

b) ◆ Physical, sexual and psychological violence occurring within the general community, including rape, sexual abuse, sexual harassment and intimidation at work, in educational institutions and elsewhere, trafficking in women and forced prostitution.

c) ◆ Physical, sexual and psychological violence perpetrated or condoned by the State, wherever it occurs. (Article 2)

CHAPTER 11

Security in areas of armed conflict

Purpose

Reducing the risks inherent in areas of armed conflict.

Risk in conflict situations

Working in conflict areas exposes human rights defenders to specific risks, especially in armed conflict situations: Many of the current killings of civilians are due to indiscriminate war making practices, and many others are due to the fact than civilians are directly targeted, and we need to recognized this as such. Political action is always needed to highlight this and try to put a halt to it.

Although you cannot exert any control over ongoing military action, you can adapt your behaviour in order to prevent being affected by the conflict or to react appropriately if something happens.

If you are established in an area where armed action occurs regularly, you will probably have developed many of the contacts necessary to protect yourself, your family and the people you work with while you try to continue working.

However, if you are working in an armed conflict area where you are not based, you must **keep three things in mind from the start**:

a ◆ What level of risk are you prepared to accept? This also applies to the individuals/organisation you are working with.

b ◆ Do the benefits of you being in the area outweigh the risks? Long-term human rights work cannot be sustained at the cost of greater exposure to high risk.

c ◆ Simply 'knowing the area' or 'knowing a lot about weapons' will not protect you if you are fired at or come under mortar or sniper attack.

The risk of coming under fire

You can be exposed to rifle and machine gun fire, mortars, rockets, bombs and missiles from land, air or sea. Fire can be more or less targeted, ranging from a sniper or helicopter in good visibility to directed mortars or artillery barrage. It can also be of the saturation variety, intended to 'pulverise' an entire area.

The more targeted the fire is, the less risk you run - as long as the fire is not directed at you, the general area you are in or a neighbouring area. In such cases the risk diminishes if you can withdraw. **In any event, remember that if you come under fire, it will be difficult to know whether you are being targeted or not. Establishing this is not a priority**, as we shall see below.

Taking precautions: Reducing your vulnerability to fire

1 ◆ Avoid dangerous places

In combat or terrorist action zones, avoid being based, having an office or remaining for long near a possible target of attack, such as a garrison or telecommunications installation. The same applies to strategic areas such as approaches to and exits from urban areas, airports or vantage points controlling the surrounding area.

2 ◆ Find adequate protection from attack

Glass flying from nearby windows is one of the main causes of injury. Boarding up windows or covering them with adhesive tape can reduce the risk of this happening. In case of attack, move away from windows and seek immediate protection on the floor, under a table or preferably in a central room with thick walls, or, even better, in a basement.

Sandbags can sometimes be useful, but only if other buildings are equipped with them too - otherwise you risk attracting unnecessary attention.

If there is nothing else available, the floor or any depression in the ground can offer at least partial protection.

A simple brick wall or car door will not protect you from rifle or heavier weapons fire. Shelling and rockets can kill at ranges up to several kilometres, so that you don't need to be very close to where the fighting is to be hit.

Bomb or mortar explosions can damage your ears: Cover them with both hands and open your mouth partially.

Obvious identification of your headquarters, location or vehicles can be useful, but be aware that **this only applies where attackers usually respect your work.** If this is not the case, you will be exposing yourselves unnecessarily. If you wish to identify yourselves, do so with a flag or colours and signals on walls and roofs (if there is a risk of air attack).

3 ◆ Travelling in vehicles

If you are in a vehicle that is being fired on directly, you can try to evaluate the situation, but making an accurate assessment in this situation is very difficult. In general, **it is useful to assume that the vehicle is or will be a target, and that the correct thing to do, therefore, is to get out and seek cover immediately.** A vehicle is a clear target. It is vulnerable, and exposes you to injuries from flying glass or exploding fuel tanks, in addition to direct fire. If the fire is not too close, try to continue travelling in the vehicle until you can take cover somewhere close at hand.

Landmines and unexploded ordnance (UXO)[1]

Landmines and unexploded ordnance pose a serious threat to civilians in armed conflict areas. They can take different forms:

☐ Mines:

◆ Anti-tank mines are laid on roads and tracks and will destroy a normal vehicle.

◆ Anti-personnel mines are smaller and can potentially be found in any place where people are supposed to pass through. Most anti-personnel mines are buried in the ground. Do not forget that people planting mines in a road may also mine the fields next to it and smaller paths nearby.

☐ Booby-traps:

◆ Booby traps are small explosives hidden in an object that looks normal or attractive, (with colours, for example), that explode when touched. The term is also used for mines linked to an object that can be moved or activated (anything from a dead body to an abandoned car).

☐ Unexploded ordnance:

◆ This refers to any type of ammunition which has been fired but has not exploded.

Prevention against mines and unexploded ordnance

The only way to avoid mined areas is to know where they are. If you are not based in or living in the area, you can only establish the location of minefields by continually and actively asking local inhabitants, or experts on the subject, if explosions or combat have occurred in the area. It is better to use asphalted highways, passable roads in regular use, and follow in the tracks made by other vehicles. **Do not leave the highway, not even onto the kerb or hard shoulder, with or without the vehicle.** Mines or other unexploded ordnance can remain hidden and active for years.

---

[1] Much of the information in this section has been adapted from Koenraad van Brabant's excellent manual, *Operational Security Management in Conflict Areas* (see the Bibliography).

Unexploded ordnance can appear in any area where combat or firing has taken place, and can be visible. The golden rule is: **Do not approach it, do not touch it, mark the spot if you can, and make it known immediately.**

Booby traps are normally found in areas which combatants have withdrawn from, In these areas it is imperative to not touch nor move anything and to stay away from abandoned buildings.

If a mine explodes underneath a nearby vehicle or person

There are two golden rules:

- Where there is one mine, there will be more.
- Never act impulsively, even though there may be people with injuries.

If you have to withdraw, retrace your steps if they are visible. If you are travelling in a vehicle and suspect there may be anti-tank mines, abandon the vehicle and withdraw by walking back along the wheel tracks.

If walking towards a victim or withdrawing from a mined area, the only way of doing so is to kneel or lie down and start prodding the ground by sticking a prodder (a very thin piece of wood or metal) carefully into the soil at a 30 degree angle, gently feeling for any hard objects. If you come upon a hard object, clear the side of it very carefully until you can see what it is. Mines can also be triggered by trip wires. Do not cut wires if you find any.

All of this can, of course, take a considerable amount of time[2].

2 You can find manuals and resources on mine awareness and education in the Web page of International Campaign to Ban Ladmines: www.icbl.org

Security, communications and information technology

(With the collaboration of Privaterra –www.privaterra.org)

Purpose

The huge gaps in information technology which exist throughout the world also affect human rights defenders. This chapter focuses mainly on information technology – i.e. computers and the internet[1]. Defenders without access to computers or the internet may not find some of the contents relevant now. Instead, they urgently need the necessary means and training to use information technology in the defence of human rights.

A guide to communications security problems and how to avoid them

Knowledge is power, and by knowing where your potential communications security problems lie, you can feel safer while doing your work. The following list outlines the various ways in which your information or communications can be illegally accessed or manipulated, and suggests ways of avoiding such security problems.

Talking

Information doesn't need to pass through the internet to be illegally accessed. When discussing sensitive issues, consider the following questions:

1 ◆ Do you trust the people you are talking to?

2 ◆ Do they need to know the information you are giving them?

3 ◆ Are you in a safe environment? Bugs or other listening devices are often specifically planted in areas where people assume they are safe, such as private offices, busy streets, home bedrooms and cars.

---

[1] This chapter is based on work done by Robert Guerra, Katitza Rodríguez y Caryn Mladen from Privaterra, an NGO which works throughout the world on security and IT for human rights defenders though courses and consultancy. Privaterra is currently working on a more detailed manual on electronic communications and security for Front Line which will be published in 2005 (this text has been slightly adapted in some parts by Enrique Eguren).

It may be difficult to know the answer to the third question, because microphones or bugs can be planted in a room to record or transmit everything being said there. Laser microphones can also be directed at windows from great distances to listen to what is being said inside a building. Heavy curtains provide some protection against laser bugs, as does installing double glazed windows. Some secure buildings have two sets of windows installed in offices to reduce the risk of laser listening devices.

What can you do?

☐ **Always assume someone is listening in.** With an attitude of healthy paranoia, you are more likely to be careful when it comes to confidential matters.

☐ **Bug sweepers or sniffers can detect listening devices,** but can be expensive and difficult to obtain. Also, sometimes the people hired to conduct the bug sweeps are responsible for the original bugging. During a sweep, they either find a few "throwaways" (cheap bugs designed to be found) or miraculously find nothing and declare your offices "clean".

☐ **Any cleaning staff could be a serious security threat.** They have after-hours access to your offices and take all your waste away with them every night. All staff should be vetted carefully for security clearance on an ongoing basis, as staff may be compromised after they join your organisation.

☐ **Change meeting rooms as often as possible.** The more rooms or places you use to discuss and exchange information, the more manpower and equipment will have to be used to listen in.

☐ **Beware of gifts designed to be kept with you at all times,** such as an expensive pen, lapel pin or broach, or used in your office, such as a beautiful paperweight or large picture. These kinds of objects have been used in the past to listen in on conversations.

☐ **Assume that some proportion of your information is compromised** at any given time. You may wish to change plans and codes often, giving your listeners only fragments of true information. Consider giving out false information to check if anyone uses or responds to it.

☐ To minimise laser microphone effectiveness, **discuss delicate matters in a basement or a room with no windows.** Some laser listening devices can be less effective during rainstorms and other atmospheric changes.

☐ **Play an audio recording of white noise or a popular song** to interfere with sound pick-up. Only expensive technology can filter out random noise to hear a conversation.

☐ **Wide open spaces can be both helpful and harmful**. Meeting in a secluded place makes it easy to see if you're being followed or observed, but makes it difficult to escape by blending in. Crowds make it easier to blend in, but far easier to be seen and heard.

Mobile phones

All phone calls can be listened into if the listener has enough technological capacity. No phone call can be assumed to be secure. Analogue mobile phones are much less secure than digital mobile phones, and both are much less secure than landlines.

Both your location and your conversations can be picked up through cellular surveillance. You don't have to be talking for your location to be tracked – this can be done anytime your mobile phone is switched on.

Do not keep information such as sensitive names and numbers in your phone's memory. If your phone is stolen, this information can be used to track down and implicate people you want to protect.

Physical security of information in the office

Keep the office locked at all times, including doors and windows. Use keys that require specific authorisation to be copied and keep track of all copies. Do NOT give keys to third parties, even maintenance and cleaning staff, and make sure you or someone you trust is always present when third parties are in the office. If this is not possible, make sure you have a room with limited access where vulnerable files are kept. Consider locking all office doors and leaving non-confidential waste outside in the hallway at night.

Use a cross-cut shredder for anything confidential. Strip shredders are mostly useless. For disposing of particularly confidential material, consider burning the shreddings, pulverizing the ashes and flushing the ashes down the toilet.

Basic computer and file security[2]

Lock computers away when leaving the office, if possible. Turn computer screens away from the windows.

Use surge protectors for all power outlets (variations in the electrical current can damage your computer).

Keep back-up information, including paper files, in a secure, separate location. Make sure your back-ups are secure by keeping them on an encrypted computer hard drive with a secure data back-up organisation, or secured by sophisticated physical locks.

To reduce the risk of someone accessing your computer, passphrase-protect your computer and always shut off your computer when you leave it.

Encrypt your files in case someone does access your computer or bypasses your passphrase protection.

---

[2] More detailed advice on computer security is available from Front Line by contacting info@frontlinedefenders.org or from Privaterra at info@privaterra.org

If your computer is stolen or destroyed, you will still be able to recover your files if you have created a secure back-up every day. Keep the encrypted back-ups away from your office in a safe place.

Erased files cannot be reconstructed if you have wiped them using PGP Wipe or another utility, instead of just placing them in the computer's trash or recycle bin.

Your computer can be programmed to send out your files or otherwise make you vulnerable without your knowledge. To avoid this, buy your computer from a trusted source, flatten the computer (i.e. reformat the hard drive) when you first get it, and then only install the software you want. Only allow trusted technicians to service your computer and watch them at all times.

Consider unplugging your computer's phone connection/modem, or otherwise physically disabling your internet connection, when leaving the machine unattended. This way, rogue programs calling out in the middle of the night will not work. Never leave your computer on when you leave for the day. Consider installing software that will disable access after a certain set time of inactivity. This way, your machine is not vulnerable while you get a coffee or make a photocopy.

In your web preferences, enable file extensions in order to tell what kind of file it is before you open it. You don't want to launch a virus by opening an executable file that you thought was a text file. In *Internet Explorer*, go to the *Tools* menu and choose *Folder Options*. Click *View* and make sure the box *Hide extensions for known file types* is NOT checked.

Internet security problems

Your email does not fly directly from your computer to the intended recipient's computer. It goes through several nodes and leaves behind information as it passes. **It can be accessed all along the path (not only in/from your country!)**

Someone could be looking over your shoulder as you type. This is especially problematic in internet cafes. If you are connected to a network, your email may be accessible to everyone else in the office. Your system administrator may have special administrative privileges to access all emails.

Your internet service provider (ISP) has access to your emails, and anyone with influence over your ISP may be able to pressure it into forwarding them copies of all your emails or to stop certain emails from getting through.

As they pass through the internet, your emails flow through hundreds of insecure third-parties. Hackers can access email messages as they pass. The ISP of your intended recipient may also be vulnerable, along with the network and office of your intended recipient.

Basic internet security

Viruses and other problems, such as Trojan Horses or Trojans, can come from anywhere; even friends may unknowingly spread viruses. Use a good anti-virus program and keep up-to-date with automatic online updating. New viruses are constantly being created and discovered, so check out the *Virus Information Library* at www.vil.nai.com for the latest virus protection patches.

Viruses are usually spread through emails, so practice safe emailing (see below). Viruses are single programs designed to replicate and may or may not be malignant. Trojans are programs designed to give a third party (or anyone!) access to your computer.

A good firewall can help you appear invisible to hackers and keep out intruders trying to get into your system. This ensures that only authorised applications can connect to the internet from your computer and prevents programs such as Trojans from sending out information or opening "back doors" to your computer through which hackers can enter.

A "key logger" system can track every keystroke you make. These programs are spread either by someone putting it onto your computer while you are away, or through a virus or Trojan that attacks your system over the internet. Key loggers track your keystrokes and report on your activities, usually over the internet. They can be defeated through passphrase-protecting your computer, practising safe emailing, using an anti-virus program, and using a mouse-guided program to type in your passphrase. Key loggers can also be disabled by physically disconnecting your computer's internet access -usually by simply unplugging the computer's telephone connection - when you are not using the computer.

An email address can be "spoofed" (faked) or used by someone other than the true owner. This can be done by obtaining access to another person's computer and password, by hacking into the service provider, or by using an address that appears to be the specific person's address. For example, by exchanging the lowercase "l" with the number "1", you can create a similar address and most people will not notice the difference. To avoid being fooled by a spoof, use meaningful subject lines and periodically ask questions that only the true person could answer. Confirm any suspicious requests for information by following it up through another form of communication.

Keep your browsing activity private by not accepting cookies and by deleting your cache after every time you use the web. In *Internet Explorer*, go to *Tools*, then *Options*. In *Netscape Navigator*, go to *Edit*, then *Preferences*. While you're in either of these menus, delete all your history, any cookies you may have and empty your cache. Remember to delete all your bookmarks as well. Browsers also keep records of the site you visit in cache files, so find out which files should be deleted on your system.

Upgrade all web browsers to support 128-bit encryption. This will help safeguard any information you want to pass securely over the web, including passwords and other sensitive data submitted on forms. Install the most recent security patches for all software used, especially *Microsoft Office, Microsoft Internet Explorer* and *Netscape*.

Don't use a computer with delicate information stored on it for non-essential web browsing.

Basic safe emailing

These are safe email practices which you and all your friends and associates should follow. Let them know that you will not open their email unless they practice safe emailing.

1 ◆ NEVER open an email from someone you don't know.

2 ◆ NEVER forward an email from someone you don't know, or which originated with someone you don't know. All those "think happy thoughts" emails that people send around could contain viruses. By sending them to your friends and associates you may be infecting their computers. If you like the sentiment enough, retype the message and send it out yourself. If retyping it is not worth your time, it's probably not that important a message.

3 ◆ NEVER download or open an attachment unless you know what it contains and that it is secure. Turn off automatic download options in your email program. Many viruses and Trojans spread themselves as "worms" and modern worms often appear to have been sent by someone you know. Smart worms scan your address book, especially if you use *Microsoft Outlook* or *Outlook Express*, and replicate by masquerading as legitimate attachments from legitimate contacts. PGP signing your emails, both with and without attachments, can greatly reduce confusion over virus-free attachments you send to colleagues (PGP is a software to encrypt information, please see below under "Encryption")

4 ◆ DON'T use HTML, MIME or rich text in your email - only plain text. Enriched emails can contain embedded programs which could allow access or damage your computer files.

5 ◆ If using *Outlook* or *Outlook Express*, turn off the preview screen option.

6 ◆ Encrypt your email whenever possible. An unencrypted email is like a postcard that can be read by anyone who sees it or obtains access to it. An encrypted email is like a letter in an envelope inside a safe.

7 ◆ Use meaningful subject lines so the reader knows that you intended to send the message. Tell all your friends and colleagues to always say something personal in the subject line so you know they truly sent the message. Otherwise someone might be spoofing them, or a Trojan might have sent out an infected program to their entire mailing list, including you. However, don't use subject lines that give away secure information in encrypted emails. Remember, the subject line is not encrypted and can give away the nature of the encrypted mail, which can trigger attacks. Many hacking programs now automatically scan and copy email messages with "interesting" subjects such as "report", "confidential" "private" and other indications that the message is of interest.

8 ◆ NEVER send email to a large group listed in the "To" or "CC" lines. Instead, send the message to yourself and include everyone else's name in the "bcc" lines. This is common courtesy as well as good privacy practice.

Otherwise, you are sending MY email address to people I don't know, a practice that is rude, offensive and potentially both frustrating and dangerous.

9 ◆ NEVER respond to spam, even to request to be taken off the list. Spam servers send email to vast hoards of addresses and they never know which ones are "live" – meaning that someone is using the email address actively. By responding, the server recognizes you as a "live" account and you are likely to receive even more spam as a result.

10 ◆ If possible, keep a separate computer, not connected to any other, that accepts general emails and contains no data files.

Encryption: Questions and Answers

The following is a list of frequently asked questions and answers. Feel free to ask us anything else you want to know by contacting the NGO Privaterra through www.privaterra.org

Q: What is encryption?

A: Encryption means scrambling data into a secret code that cannot be deciphered except by the intended party. Given enough time and computing power, all encrypted messages can be read, but this can take huge amounts of time and resources. In simple terms, encryption is a way for you to secure your files and emails from spying eyes. Your files get translated into code – an apparently random collection of numbers and letters - that makes no sense to anyone who sees it.. To encrypt a file, you "lock" it with a key, represented by a pass phrase. To encrypt a message, you lock it with a key pair using your pass phrase. It can only be opened by the intended recipient, using his or her own pass phrase.

Q: Why should human rights groups use encryption?

A: Everyone should use encryption, because digital communications are inherently unsafe. However, human rights workers are much more at risk than most people and their files and communications are more sensitive. It is imperative for human rights workers to use encryption to protect themselves and the people they are trying to help.

Digital technology is a benefit to human rights groups, allowing them easier communications, greater efficiency and more opportunities. However, with any benefits come certain dangers. Just because you wear a seat belt doesn't mean you are expected to have an accident every time you drive. Driving in a more dangerous situation, such as a race, makes you even more likely to use a seatbelt, just to be safe.

Human rights workers are known targets of surveillance. Since unencrypted emails can be accessed and read by almost anyone, it is almost inevitable that your unencrypted emails will be accessed at some point. Your messages may already be monitored by your opponents and you will never know. The opponents of people you are working to help are also your opponents.

Q: Is it illegal to use encryption?

A: Sometimes. It is perfectly legal to use encryption in most countries of the world. However, there are exceptions. In China, for example, organisations must apply for a permit to use encryption, and any encryption technology on your laptop must be declared as you enter the country. Singapore and Malaysia have laws requiring anyone wishing to use encryption to report their private keys. Similar laws are pending in India. Other exceptions also exist.

The Electronic Privacy Information Center (EPIC) provides an *International Survey of Encryption Policy* discussing the laws in most countries at http://www2.epic.org/reports/crypto2000/. This list was last updated in 2000. If you are concerned check with Privaterra before using encryption in a particular country.

Q: What do we need to keep our IT systems safe?

A: It depends on your system and your activities, but generally everyone should have:

- A firewall.
- Disk encryption.
- Email encryption that also does digital signatures such as PGP.
- Virus detection software.
- Secure back-up: Email all materials to a secure site and do weekly back-ups to CD-RW. Then store it at a separate, secure location.
- Passphrases that can be remembered but not guessed.
- A hierarchy of access – everyone in the organisation does not need access to all files.
- Consistency – none of the tools will work if you don't use them all the time!

But having the right software is not the whole solution. **Individuals are usually the weakest link, not technology.** Encryption doesn't work if individuals don't use it consistently, if they share their passphrases indiscriminately or make them visible, for example, on a sticky note pasted to their monitors. Back-up software won't save you in the event of a fire or raid if you don't keep the back-up copy at a separate, secure location. Sensitive information must be treated on a need-to-know basis instead of being shared with everyone in organisation, so you need to create hierarchies and protocols. In general, it's important to be conscious of privacy and security in your everyday activities. We call this "healthy paranoia".

Q: How do I choose which encryption software to use?

A: Usually, you can ask your friends - and confirm with us. You need to communicate with certain people and groups, so if they are using a specific encryption system, you should use it too to facilitate communications. However, check with us first. Some software packages simply don't do a good job, while others are honey pots. Honey pots lure you into using free and seemingly excellent software provided by the very people who want to spy on you. How better to read your most vulnerable communications than by being the overseer of your encryption software? Still, there are many reputable brands of both proprietary software and freeware - just remember to investigate before you use it[3].

Q: Won't using encryption put me at a greater risk of a crackdown?

A: No one will know you are using encryption unless your email traffic is already being watched. If so, your private information is already being read. That means you are already involved in a crackdown by those doing surveillance on you. There is a concern that those doing surveillance on you will use other options if they can no longer read your emails, so it is important to know your colleagues and implement safe back-up policies and consistent office management at the same time as when you begin to use encryption.

(Note: We have no information from cases in which the use of encryption software has caused problems to defenders. However, consider this possibility carefully before starting encryption, specially if you are in a country with a heavy armed conflict –military intelligence could suspect that you may pass relevant information from the military point of view- or if very few defender use encryption –this could attract unwanted attention on you).

Q: Why do we need to encrypt emails and documents all the time?

A: If you only use encryption for delicate matters, those watching you or your clients can guess when critical activity is taking place, and become more likely to crack down at those times. While they cannot read your encrypted communications, they can tell whether files are encrypted or not. A sudden rise in encryption may trigger a raid, so it is a good idea to start using encryption before special projects begin. In fact, it's best to ensure all communication traffic flows smoothly. Send encrypted emails at regular intervals, even when there is nothing new to report. This way, when you need to send delicate information, it will be less noticeable.

Q: If I've got a firewall, why do I need to encrypt my email?

A: Firewalls prevent hackers from accessing your hard drive and network but, once you send an email into the internet, it is open to the world. You need to protect it before you send it.

Q: No one is breaking into my office, so why should I use privacy software?

A: You don't know if someone is breaking into your system or leaking information. Without encrypted communications, physical security or privacy protocols, anyone can be accessing your files, reading your emails and manipulating your documents without your knowledge. Your open communications can also put others at risk in places where politically motivated raids are more likely to happen. If you lock your doors, you should encrypt your files. It's that simple.

---

[3] For example, PGP –"Pretty Good Privacy"- is a well-known and safe one. You can download it from www.pgpi.org

Q: We don't have internet access and have to use an internet café. How can we protect communications sent from an outside computer?

A: You can still encrypt your emails and your files. Before going to the internet café, encrypt any files you intend to email and copy them in encrypted form onto your floppy disk or CD. At the internet café, sign up for an encryption service such as www.hushmail.com or an anonymity service such as www.anonymizer.com, and use these when sending your emails. Make sure the people receiving your communications have signed up for these services too.

Q: If it is that important to secure our files and communications, why doesn't everyone do it?

A: This technology is relatively new, but its usage is spreading. Banks, multinational corporations, news agencies and governments all use encryption, seeing it as a sound investment and a necessary cost of doing business. NGOs are at greater risk than companies, which most governments welcome. NGOs are more likely targets of surveillance and therefore need to be proactive in implementing the technology. Human rights workers are concerned with protecting persecuted individuals and groups. To do so, they keep files which can identify and locate people. If these files are accessed, these individuals can be killed, tortured, kidnapped, or "persuaded" not to assist the NGO anymore. Information from these files can also be used as evidence against the NGO and their clients in political prosecutions.

Q: One of our principles is openness. We are lobbying for greater government transparency. How can we use privacy technology?

A: Privacy is consistent with openness. If the government wishes to openly request your files, it can do so through proper and recognised procedures. Privacy technology stops people from accessing your information in a clandestine way.

Q: We follow all the privacy and security protocols and our information is still leaked – what's going on?

A: You may have a spy within your organisation or someone who simply cannot keep information confidential. Rework your information hierarchy to ensure fewer people have access to delicate information – and keep an especially watchful eye on those few people. Large corporations and organisations routinely disseminate different bits of false information to specific people as a matter or course. If this false information leaks out, the leak can be tracked directly back to the employee who was given the original, false information.

Dos and don'ts of using encryption

☐ **DO** use encryption consistently. If you only encrypt sensitive material, anyone monitoring your email traffic will know when something important is about to happen. A sudden increase in use of encryption might lead to a raid.

☐ **DON'T** put sensitive information in subject lines. They are usually not encrypted, even if the message is.

□ **DO** use a pass phrase containing letters, numbers, spacing and punctuation that only you can remember. Some techniques for safe pass phrase creation are using designs on your keyboard or random words strung together with symbols in between. In general, the longer the pass phrase, the stronger it is.

□ **DON'T** use a single word, name, popular phrase or an address in your address book for your pass phrase. These can be cracked in minutes.

□ **DO** back-up your private key (the file that contents your private key for encryption software) in a single secure place, such as encrypted on a floppy disk or on a tiny, removable "keychain" USB memory device).

□ **DON'T** send sensitive material to someone just because they've sent you an encrypted email using a recognisable name. Anyone can "spoof" a name by making his or her email address sound like someone you know. Always verify someone's identity before trusting the source – communicate in person, check by phone, or send another email to double-check.

□ **DO** teach others to use encryption. The more people are using it, the safer we will all be.

□ **DON'T** forget to sign the message as well as encrypting it. You want your recipient to know whether your message has been changed in transit.

□ **DO** encrypt files sent as separate attachments. They are generally not automatically encrypted when you send an encrypted email.

A guide to safer office and information management

Safer Office Management

Safer office management is about creating habits. Office management habits can be useful or harmful. To develop useful office management habits, it helps to understand the reasoning behind them. We've put together lists of habits that can help you manage your information more safely – but only if you develop these habits and think about why they are important.

What is most important for privacy and security in office management?

- Being conscious of your information and who has access to it
- Developing safe habits and using them consistently
- Using the tools properly

Administration

Many organisations have a system administrator or someone who has administrative privileges to access email, network computers and oversee installation of new software. If someone leaves the organisation or is unavailable, the administrator can then access the individual's information and business can continue uninterrupted. Also, this means someone is responsible for ensuring that the system software is clean and from a reputable source.

The problem is that some organisations consider this role merely as technical support and allow a third party contractor to hold administrative privileges. This administrator has effective control over all information in the organisation, and must therefore be absolutely trustworthy. Some organisations share the administrator role between the head of the organisation and another trusted individual.

Some organisations choose to collect PGP private keys and passwords, encrypt and store them securely and remotely with another trusted organisation. This prevents problems if individuals forget their password or lose their private key. However, the location where the files are kept must be absolutely secure and trustworthy, and specific and extensive protocols must be created relating to accessing the files.

The rules:

1 ◆ NEVER give administrative privileges to a third party contractor. Not only are they less trustworthy than people within the organisation, but someone outside the office may also be difficult to reach in emergencies.

2 ◆ Only the most trustworthy individuals should have administrative privileges.

3 ◆ Determine how much information should be accessible by the administrator: Access to all computers, computer pass phrases, login pass phrases, PGP keys and pass phrases, etc.

4 ◆ If you choose to keep copies of pass phrases and PGP private keys with another organisation, you must develop protocols for access.

5 ◆ If an individual leaves the organisation, his or her individual pass phrases and access codes should be changed immediately.

6 ◆ If someone with administrative privileges leaves the organization, all pass phrases and access codes should be changed immediately.

Software administration

Using pirated software can leave an organisation vulnerable to what we call the "software police". Officials can crack down on an organisation for using illegal software, imposing huge fines and effectively shutting them down. The organisation in question gets little sympathy or support from Western media because this is not seen as an attack on a human rights NGO, but as an attack on piracy. Be extremely careful about your software licenses and do not allow software to be randomly copied by anyone in the office. Pirated software may also be insecure because it can contain viruses. Always use an anti-virus utility whenever software is being installed.

An administrator should have control over new software being installed to ensure that it is checked first. Do not allow installation of potentially insecure software, and only install software that is necessary.

Install the most recent security patches for all software used, especially *Microsoft Office, Microsoft Internet Explorer* and *Netscape*. The biggest threat to security lies within software and hardware delivered with known vulnerabilities. Better yet, consider switching to *Open Source* software, which doesn't rely on the "Security through Obscurity" model, but rather welcomes security experts and hackers alike to rigorously test all code. Using *Open Source* software and any software other than Microsoft has the added benefit of making you less vulnerable to standard viruses and non-specific hackers. Fewer viruses are created for Linux or Macintosh operating systems because most people use Windows. *Outlook* is the most popular email program, and therefore the most popular target for hackers.

Email habits

Email encryption should become a habit. It is easier to remember to encrypt everything than to have a policy of when email should be encrypted and when it should not. Remember, if email is always encrypted, no one watching your traffic will ever know when your communications become more significant and delicate.

A few other important points:

☐ Always save encrypted email in encrypted form. You can always decrypt it again later, but if someone gains access to your computer, it is just as vulnerable as if it had never been encrypted.

☐ Be persistent with everyone with whom you exchange encrypted emails to make sure they do not decrypt and forward emails, or reply without bothering to encrypt them. Individual laziness is the biggest threat to your communications.

☐ You might wish to create a few safe email accounts for people in the field that are not generally used and so do not get picked up by spam servers. These addresses should be checked consistently but not used, except by field staff. This way you can destroy email addresses that are getting a lot of spam without endangering your contact base.

General tips for internet cafés and beyond

Emails sent in plain text or unencrypted across the internet can be read by many different parties, if they make the effort to do so. One of these may be your local Internet Service Provider (ISP) or any ISP through which your emails pass. An email travels through many computers to get from the sender to the recipient; it ignores geopolitical boundaries and may pass through another country's servers even if you are sending emails within the same country.

Some general tips on issues commonly misunderstood by internet users:

☐ Password-protecting a file does so little to protect the file that it is not worth doing for documents containing sensitive information. It only provides a false sense of security.

109

□ Zipping a file does not protect it from anyone wanting to see what is inside.

□ If you want to make sure a file or email is sent securely, use encryption (see www.privaterra.com).

□ If you want to send an email or a document securely, use encryption all the way to the final recipient. It is not good enough to send an encrypted email from a field office to New York or London or anywhere else and then have that same email forwarded unencrypted to another person.

□ The internet is global in nature. There is no difference between sending an email between two offices in Manhattan and sending an email from an internet café in South Africa to a London office computer.

□ Use encryption as often as possible, even if the email or data you are sending are not sensitive!

□ Make sure the computer you are using has virus protection software. Many viruses are written to extract information from your computer, whether it be your hard drive contents or you email files, including email address books.

□ Make sure your software is properly licensed. If you are using unlicensed software, you instantly become a software pirate instead of a human rights activist in the eyes of governments and media. The best option is to use open source software – it's free!

□ There is no 100% secure solution if you are using the internet. Be aware that a person can "socially hack" into a system by pretending to be some-one they are not on the phone or by email. Use your own judgement and common sense.

The UN Declaration on Human Rights Defenders

UNITED

NATIONS

A

General Assembly

Distr.
GENERAL

A/RES/53/144
8 March 1999

Fifty-third session
Agenda item 110 (*b*)

RESOLUTION ADOPTED BY THE GENERAL ASSEMBLY

[*on the report of the Third Committee (A/53/625/Add.2)*]

53/144. **Declaration on the Right and Responsibility of Individuals, Groups and Organs of Society to Promote and Protect Universally Recognized Human Rights and Fundamental Freedoms**

The General Assembly,

Reaffirming the importance of the observance of the purposes and principles of the Charter of the United Nations for the promotion and protection of all human rights and fundamental freedoms for all persons in all countries of the world,

Taking note of Commission on Human Rights resolution 1998/7 of 3 April 1998,[1] in which the Commission approved the text of the draft declaration on the right and responsibility of individuals, groups and organs of society to promote and protect universally recognized human rights and fundamental freedoms,

Taking note also of Economic and Social Council resolution 1998/33 of 30 July 1998, in which the Council recommended the draft declaration to the General Assembly for adoption, *Conscious* of the importance of the adoption of the draft declaration in the context of the fiftieth anniversary of the Universal Declaration of Human Rights,[2]

1. *Adopts* the Declaration on the Right and Responsibility of Individuals, Groups and Organs of Society to Promote and Protect Universally Recognized Human Rights and Fundamental Freedoms, annexed to the present resolution;

2. *Invites* Governments, agencies and organizations of the United Nations system and intergovernmental and non-governmental organizations to intensify their efforts to disseminate the Declaration and to promote universal respect and understanding there of, and requests the Secretary-General to include the text of the Declaration in the next edition of *Human Rights: A Compilation of International Instruments.*

85th plenary meeting
9 December 1998

Declaration on the Right and Responsibility of Individuals, Groups and Organs of Society to Promote and Protect Universally Recognized Human Rights and Fundamental Freedoms

The General Assembly,

Reaffirming the importance of the observance of the purposes and principles of the Charter of the United Nations for the promotion and protection of all human rights and fundamental freedoms for all persons in all countries of the world,

Reaffirming also the importance of the Universal Declaration of Human Rights[2] and the International Covenants on Human Rights[3] as basic elements of international efforts to promote universal respect for and observance of human rights and fundamental freedoms and the importance of other human rights instruments adopted within the United Nations system, as well as those at the regional level,

Stressing that all members of the international community shall fulfil, jointly and separately, their solemn obligation to promote and encourage respect for human rights and fundamental freedoms for all without distinction of any kind, including distinctions based on race, colour, sex, language, religion, political or other opinion, national or social origin, property, birth or other status, and reaffirming the particular importance of achieving international cooperation to fulfil this obligation according to the Charter,

---

[1] See *Official Records of the Economic and Social Council, 1998, Supplement No. 3* (E/1998/23), chap. II, sect. A.
[2] Resolution 217 A (III).
[3] Resolution 2200 A (XXI), annex.

Acknowledging the important role of international cooperation for, and the valuable work of individuals, groups and associations in contributing to, the effective elimination of all violations of human rights and fundamental freedoms of peoples and individuals, including in relation to mass, flagrant or systematic violations such as those resulting from apartheid, all forms of racial discrimination, colonialism, foreign domination or occupation, aggression or threats to national sovereignty, national unity or territorial integrity and from the refusal to recognize the right of peoples to self-determination and the right of every people to exercise full sovereignty over its wealth and natural resources,

Recognizing the relationship between international peace and security and the enjoyment of human rights and fundamental freedoms, and mindful that the absence of international peace and security does not excuse non-compliance,

Reiterating that all human rights and fundamental freedoms are universal, indivisible, interdependent and interrelated and should be promoted and implemented in a fair and equitable manner, without prejudice to the implementation of each of those rights and freedoms,

Stressing that the prime responsibility and duty to promote and protect human rights and fundamental freedoms lie with the State,

Recognizing the right and the responsibility of individuals, groups and associations to promote respect for and foster knowledge of human rights and fundamental freedoms at the national and international levels,

Declares:

Article 1

Everyone has the right, individually and in association with others, to promote and to strive for the protection and realization of human rights and fundamental freedoms at the national and international levels.

Article 2

1.   Each State has a prime responsibility and duty to protect, promote and implement all human rights and fundamental freedoms, *inter alia*, by adopting such steps as may be necessary to create all conditions necessary in the social, economic, political and other fields, as well as the legal guarantees required to ensure that all persons under its jurisdiction, individually and in association with others, are able to enjoy all those rights and freedoms in practice.

2.   Each State shall adopt such legislative, administrative and other steps as may be necessary to ensure that the rights and freedoms referred to in the present Declaration are effectively guaranteed.

Article 3

3.   Domestic law consistent with the Charter of the United Nations and other international obligations of the State in the field of human rights and fundamental freedoms is the juridical framework within which human rights and fundamental freedoms should be implemented and enjoyed and within which all activities referred to in the present Declaration for the promotion, protection and effective realization of those rights and freedoms should be conducted.

Article 4

Nothing in the present Declaration shall be construed as impairing or contradicting the purposes and principles of the Charter of the United Nations or as restricting or derogating from the provisions of the Universal Declaration of Human Rights,[2] the International Covenants on Human Rights[3] and other international instruments and commitments applicable in this field.

Article 5

For the purpose of promoting and protecting human rights and fundamental freedoms, everyone has the right, individually and in association with others, at the national and international levels:

(*a*) To meet or assemble peacefully;

(*b*) To form, join and participate in non-governmental organizations, associations or groups;

(*c*) To communicate with non-governmental or intergovernmental organizations.

Article 6

Everyone has the right, individually and in association with others:

(*a*) To know, seek, obtain, receive and hold information about all human rights and fundamental freedoms, including having access to information as to how those rights and freedoms are given effect in domestic legislative, judicial or administrative systems;

(*b*) As provided for in human rights and other applicable international instruments, freely to publish, impart or disseminate to others views, information and knowledge on all human rights and fundamental freedoms;

(*c*) To study, discuss, form and hold opinions on the observance, both in law and in practice, of all human rights and fundamental freedoms and, through these and other appropriate means, to draw public attention to those matters.

Article 7

Everyone has the right, individually and in association with others, to develop and discuss new human rights ideas and principles and to advocate their acceptance.

Article 8

1.   Everyone has the right, individually and in association with others, to have effective access, on a non-discriminatory basis, to participation in the government of his or her country and in the conduct of public affairs.

2.   This includes, *inter alia*, the right, individually and in association with others, to submit to governmental bodies and agencies and organizations concerned with public affairs criticism and proposals for improving their functioning and to draw attention to any aspect of their work that may hinder or impede the promotion, protection and realization of human rights and fundamental freedoms.

Article 9

1.   In the exercise of human rights and fundamental freedoms, including the promotion and protection of human rights as referred to in the present Declaration, everyone has the right, individually and in association with others, to benefit from an effective remedy and to be protected in the event of the violation of those rights.

2.   To this end, everyone whose rights or freedoms are allegedly violated has the right, either in person or through legally authorized representation, to complain to and have that complaint promptly reviewed in a public hearing before an independent, impartial and competent judicial or other authority established by law and to obtain from such an authority a decision, in accordance with law, providing redress, including any compensation due, where there has been a violation of that person's rights or freedoms, as well as enforcement of the eventual decision and award, all without undue delay.

3.   To the same end, everyone has the right, individually and in association with others, *inter alia*:

(*a*)   To complain about the policies and actions of individual officials and governmental bodies with regard to violations of human rights and fundamental freedoms, by petition or other appropriate means, to competent domestic judicial, administrative or legislative authorities or any other competent authority provided for by the legal system of the State, which should render their decision on the complaint without undue delay;

(*b*)   To attend public hearings, proceedings and trials so as to form an opinion on their compliance with national law and applicable international obligations and commitments;

(*c*)   To offer and provide professionally qualified legal assistance or other relevant advice and assistance in defending human rights and fundamental freedoms.

4.   To the same end, and in accordance with applicable international instruments and procedures, everyone has the right, individually and in association with others, to unhindered access to and communication with international bodies with general or special competence to receive and consider communications on matters of human rights and fundamental freedoms.

5.   The State shall conduct a prompt and impartial investigation or ensure that an inquiry takes place whenever there is reasonable ground to believe that a violation of human rights and fundamental freedoms has occurred in any territory under its jurisdiction.

Article 10

No one shall participate, by act or by failure to act where required, in violating human rights and fundamental freedoms and no one shall be subjected to punishment or adverse action of any kind for refusing to do so.

Article 11

Everyone has the right, individually and in association with others, to the lawful exercise of his or her occupation or profession. Everyone who, as a result of his or her profession, can affect the human dignity, human rights and fundamental freedoms of others should respect those rights and freedoms and comply with relevant national and international standards of occupational and professional conduct or ethics.

Article 12

1.   Everyone has the right, individually and in association with others, to participate in peaceful activities against violations of human rights and fundamental freedoms.

2.   The State shall take all necessary measures to ensure the protection by the competent authorities of everyone, individually and in association with others, against any violence, threats, retaliation, de facto or *de jure* adverse discrimination, pressure or any other arbitrary action as a consequence of his or her legitimate exercise of the rights referred to in the present Declaration.

3.   In this connection, everyone is entitled, individually and in association with others, to be protected effectively under national law in reacting against or opposing, through peaceful means, activities and acts, including those by omission, attributable to States that result in violations of human rights and fundamental freedoms, as well as acts of violence perpetrated by groups or individuals that affect the enjoyment of human rights and fundamental freedoms.

Article 13

Everyone has the right, individually and in association with others, to solicit, receive and utilize resources for the express purpose of promoting and protecting human rights and fundamental freedoms through peaceful means, in accordance with article 3 of the present Declaration.

Article 14

1.   The State has the responsibility to take legislative, judicial, administrative or other appropriate measures to promote the understanding by all persons under its jurisdiction of their civil, political, economic, social and cultural rights.

2.   Such measures shall include, *inter alia*:

(*a*) The publication and widespread availability of national laws and regulations and of applicable basic international human rights instruments;

(*b*) Full and equal access to international documents in the field of human rights, including the periodic reports by the State to the bodies established by the international human rights treaties to which it is a party, as well as the summary records of discussions and the official reports of these bodies.

3.   The State shall ensure and support, where appropriate, the creation and development of further independent national institutions for the promotion and protection of human rights and fundamental freedoms in all territory under its jurisdiction, whether they be ombudsmen, human rights commissions or any other form of national institution.

Article 15

The State has the responsibility to promote and facilitate the teaching of human rights and fundamental freedoms at all levels of education and to ensure that all those responsible for training lawyers, law enforcement officers, the personnel of the armed forces and public officials include appropriate elements of human rights teaching in their training programme.

Article 16

Individuals, non-governmental organizations and relevant institutions have an important role to play in contributing to making the public more aware of questions relating to all human rights and fundamental freedoms through activities such as education, training and research in these areas to strengthen further, *inter alia*, understanding, tolerance, peace and friendly relations among nations and among all racial and religious groups, bearing in mind the various backgrounds of the societies and communities in which they carry out their activities.

Article 17

In the exercise of the rights and freedoms referred to in the present Declaration, everyone, acting individually and in association with others, shall be subject only to such limitations as are in accordance with applicable international obligations and are determined by law solely for the purpose of securing due recognition and respect for the rights and freedoms of others and of meeting the just requirements of morality, public order and the general welfare in a democratic society.

Article 18

1.   Everyone has duties towards and within the community, in which alone the free and full development of his or her personality is possible.

2.   Individuals, groups, institutions and non-governmental organizations have an important role to play and a responsibility in safeguarding democracy, promoting human rights and fundamental freedoms and contributing to the promotion and advancement of democratic societies, institutions and processes.

3.   Individuals, groups, institutions and non-governmental organizations also have an important role and a responsibility in contributing, as appropriate, to the promotion of the right of everyone to a social and international order in which the rights and freedoms set forth in the Universal Declaration of Human Rights and other human rights instruments can be fully realized.

Article 19

Nothing in the present Declaration shall be interpreted as implying for any individual, group or organ of society or any State the right to engage in any activity or to perform any act aimed at the destruction of the rights and freedoms referred to in the present Declaration.

Article 20

Nothing in the present Declaration shall be interpreted as permitting States to support and promote activities of individuals, groups of individuals, institutions or non-governmental organizations contrary to the provisions of the Charter of the United Nations.

Selected bibliography and additional resources

SELECTED BIBLIOGRAPHY

◆ Amnesty International (2003): "Essential actors of our time. Human rights defenders in the Americas". AI International Secretariat (Index AI: AMR 01/009/2003/s)

◆ AVRE and ENS (2002): "Afrontar la amenaza por persecución sindical". Escuela de Liderazgo Sindical Democrático. Published by the Escuela Nacional Sindical and Corporación AVRE. Medellín, Colombia.

◆ Bettocchi, G., Cabrera, A.G., Crisp, J., and Varga, A (2002): "Protection and solutions in situations of internal displacement". EPAU/2002/10, UNHCR.

◆ Cohen, R. (1996): "Protecting the Internally Displaced". World Refugee Survey.

◆ Conway, T., Moser, C., Norton, A. and Farrington, J. (2002) "Rights and livelihoods approaches: Exploring policy dimensions". DFID Natural Resource Perspectives, no. 78. ODI, London.

◆ Dworken, J.T "Threat assessment". Series of modules for OFDA/InterAction PVO Security Task Force (Mimeo, included in REDR Security Training Modules, 2001).

◆ Eguren, E. (2000): "Who should go where? Examples from Peace Brigades International", in "Peacebuilding: a Field Perspective. A Handbook for Field Diplomats", by Luc Reychler and Thania Paffenholz (editors). Lynne Rienner Publishers (London).

◆ Eguren, E. (2000), "The Protection Gap: Policies and Strategies" in the ODI HPN Report, London: Overseas Development Institute.

◆ Eguren, E. (2000), "Beyond security planning: Towards a model of security management. Coping with the security challenges of the humanitarian work". Journal of Humanitarian Assistance. Bradford, UK. www.jha.ac/articles/a060.pdf

◆ Eriksson, A. (1999) "Protecting internally displaced persons in Kosovo". http://web.mit.edu/cis/www/migration/kosovo.html#f4

◆ ICRC (1983): Fundamental Norms of Geneva Conventions and Additional Protocols. Geneva.

◆ International Council on Human Rights Policy (2002): "Ends and means: Human Rights Approaches to Armed Groups". Versoix (Switzerland). www.international-council.org

◆ Jacobsen, K. (1999) "A 'Safety-First' Approach to Physical Protection in Refugee Camps". Working Paper # 4 (mimeo).

◆ Jamal, A. (2000): "Acces to safety? Negotiating protection in a Central Asia emergency. Evaluation and Policy Analysis Unit, UNHCR. Geneva.

◆ Lebow, Richard Ned and Gross Stein, Janice. (1990) "When Does Deterrence Succeed And How Do We Know?" (Occasional Paper 8). Ottawa: Canadian Inst. for Peace and International Security.

◆ Mahony, L. and Eguren, E. (1997): "Unarmed bodyguards. International accompaniment for the protection of human rights". Kumarian Press. West Hartford, CT (USA).

◆ Martin Beristain, C. and Riera, F. (1993): "Afirmacion y resistencia. La comunidad como apoyo". Virus Editorial. Barcelona.

◆ Paul, Diane (1999): "Protection in practice: Field level strategies for protecting civilians from deliberate harm". ODI Network Paper no. 30.

◆ SEDEM (2000): Manual de Seguridad. Seguridad en Democracia. Guatemala.

◆ Slim, H. and Eguren, E. (2003): "Humanitarian Protection: An ALNAP guidance booklet". ALNAP. www.alnap.org.uk. London.

◆ Sustainable Livelihoods Guidance Sheets (2000). DFID. London, February 2000

◆ Sutton, R. (1999) The policy process: An overview. Working Paper 118. ODI. London.

◆ UNHCHR (2004): "About Human Rights Defenders" (extensive information): http://www.unhchr.ch/defenders/about1.htm

◆ UNHCHR (2004): "Human Rights Defenders: Protecting the Right to Defend Human Rights". Fact Sheet no. 29. Geneva.

◆ UNHCHR (2004): On women defenders: www.unhchr.ch/defenders/tiwomen.htm

◆ UNHCR (1999): Protecting Refugees: A Field Guide for NGO. Geneva.

◆ UNHCR (2001): Complementary forms of protection. Global Consultations on International Protection. EC/GC/01/18 4 September 2001

◆ UNHCR (2002) Strengthening protection capacities in host countries. Global Consultations on International Protection. EC/GC/01/19 * / 19 April 2002

◆ UNHCR-Department of Field Protection (2002) Designing protection strategies and measuring progress: Checklist for UNHCR staff. Mimeo. Geneva.

◆ Van Brabant, Koenraad (2000): "Operational Security Managment in Violent Environments". Good Practice Review 8. Humanitarian Practice Network. Overseas Development Institute, London.

◆ Vincent, M. and Sorensen, B. (eds) (2001) "Caught between borders. Response strategies of the internally displaced". Pluto Press. London.

ADDITIONAL RESOURCES

The European Office of Peace Brigades International provides trainings and advice on protection and security for human rights defenders since 2000, depending on time and resources available for it.

Please contact pbibeo@biz.tiscali.be, or write to PBI- European Office, 38, Rue Saint-Christophe, 1000 Bruxelles (Belgium)
Phone/fax + 32 (0)2 511 14 98
www.peacebrigades.org/beo.html

Front Line supports training and capacity building in security and protection for human rights defenders and produces related manuals and materials.

For further information check www.frontlinedefenders.org or contact info@frontlinedefenders.org or write to Front Line, 16 Idrone lane, Off Bath Place, Blackrock, County Dublin, Ireland
tel: +353 1212 3750 fax: +353 1212 1001

Thematic Index

For my son Thomas with love and thanks

Table of Contents

POEMS

FOR THE AUTUMN TERM

SUMMER HAS GONE

Summer has gone and the rain's coming down,
There's a definite nip in the air,
It's dark in the mornings when I go to school
And I really don't think it's fair.
Why can't we have sunny days all through the year
And skies that are blue and bright?
With plenty of time to enjoy the fresh air
And evenings still warm and light?
I don't want to have to go back to my work,
I don't want homework and sums.
I'll just have to do it though, I suppose,
And wait until Christmas comes!

AUTUMN

I'm told to write about crispy leaves,
And waving golden harvest sheaves,
Or fruit that's glowing on the tree,
But that sort of poem isn't me.

I'll write about the wild grey sea,
With waves that rise up angrily
And wind blown beaches, driven sand
As Winter starts to own the land.

Teacher talks about crusty bread
And berries black and apples red,
The turning colours of the tree,
But that sort of poem isn't me.

I'll write about hailstorms driving by
The stark bare trees against grey sky,
The fog that swirls, the frost that bites,
The early dark of the longer nights.

Lightning squiggles like silver wire,
The welcome of curling up by the fire,
The relentless rattling of driving rain
And between me and Autumn, the window pane!

STARS

There are no stars on a stormy night
When the clouds are driven by
Across the face of the watery moon
And a rain streaked sky.

But when the air is calm and still
On a dark and silent night,
There in the sky are millions of stars
Twinkling high and bright.

I think that there's one that shines for me
Brighter than others by far.
I look at it and tell my dreams
To my special wishing star.

I hope it will make them all come true
For it seems to wink its eye
And I know that my star is always there
Up in the sky so high.

WET

I've been out in the rain today, and I bet
That nobody ever got quite so wet!
My shoes they squelch
Cos I stepped in a puddle
And my socks are sodden,
(That could mean trouble).
The drops from my hood have dripped down my
neck
And my anorak is simply a soggy wreck.
My trousers are soaked through to my knees
And they flap like sails in stormy seas.
My gloves are as cold and damp as can be;
No – nobody's ever been wetter than me!

THE HALLOWEEN PARTY

I wanted to go to the Halloween Party,
I was going to go as a witch,
But Sarah said lots of people were witches
And they wouldn't know which witch was which.
So I thought I might go as a witch's familiar
A mystical coal black cat,
I could wear a furry coat of my mums
But Pat said I'd be too hot in that!
Then I thought that I might be a ghost
In a sheet with two holes for my eyes,
But Miranda said nobody'd know it was me
So I wouldn't win the best prize.
So now I don't want to go there at all
And I'm having a sulk and a wail
Till Mum says, "You're a little demon tonight,
All you need is some horns and a tail!"

GHOSTLY GOINGS ON

There are ghostly goings on at number forty four,
The tables and the chairs have risen from the floor,
The pictures on the walls have moved to places new,
And in the dark at night has been heard a "Whoo!
Whoo!"

There's a creepy feeling as you tread the stair,
So don't look behind you in case there's someone there.
There's an icy breath and a chilling whisper too,
That seems to say, "I've got my beady eye on you".

That faint light in the distance – could it be a spook?
I just freeze with fear and cannot bear to look.
Now it's looming closer like a great grisly beast –
Sorry Dad, but I just felt like a midnight feast!

THE ROCKET

The night was so dark and the wind was cold,
The lights from the house shone out warm and gold,
My dad took the box out onto the grass
And put the rocket to stand in a glass.
"Keep back", he said, "It's a dangerous game",
As he lit the touchpaper with a flame.
It sizzled and hissed with an orange glow,
Then our eyes lit up as we watched it go
Shooting and squealing out into the night,
Exploding with stars that sparkled so bright.
It dazzled the sky and outshone the stars
Like a glittering fountain falling fast,
Cascading in streams with a golden spray;
Then the beautiful rocket died away.
But the magic stayed with me of what I'd seen
And the rocket soared again in that night's dream.

FIREWORKS

Remember, remember the fifth of November
For that's when we light up the night
With rockets and wheels and shooting stars
And suddenly, everything's bright.
The children all stand with faces upturned
As the sparklers reflect in their eyes,
And smiles as wide as a comet's tail
Greet each new exploding surprise.
The air grows thick with swirling smoke
And that FIZZ! BANG! WHOOSH! Beats the lot.
Yes, this is the season
When gunpowder treason
Is certainly never forgot!

Eleanor McLeod

HARVEST

Purple of berries and gold of the sheaves,
Red of the apples and brown of the leaves,
These are the colours of Harvest.

Bubble of jams and a sweet apple pie
Roasting of chestnuts with smoke in the sky
These are the scents of the Harvest.

Rustle of Squirrel hiding his load,
Rattle of tractor taking hay down the road,
These are the sounds of the Harvest.

Bringing of gifts to the school Harvest table,
Giving to others what we are able,
These are the joys of the Harvest.

BRING THE HARVEST HOME

Bring the Harvest home,
Oh bring the Harvest home
To lands where earth is parched and dry
And hungry children daily cry,
Let us send what help we may
That they with hope will say one day,
We've brought the Harvest home.

Bring the Harvest home,
Oh bring the Harvest home
To those nearby who are in need
And if in love we plant a seed
We'll reap the grains of joy and care
To show that we have learnt to share
And brought the Harvest home.

Bring the Harvest home,
Oh bring the Harvest home,
For we have much and life is good,
While others pray for daily food
So let us join to gladly give
That they might take, that they might live
And bring the Harvest home.

Eleanor McLeod

THE MESSAGE OF CHRISTMAS

What is the message of Christmas,
What does it mean to you?
A couple of humble shepherd's kneeling
And a star or two?

A wooden manger heaped with straw
And ox and ass around,
Three foreign kings with wealth and power,
Precious gifts and gilded crowns.

The shops crammed full of costly things
That no-one really needs,
The churches full of those we see
Only on Christmas Eve.

A white robed angel singing,
A choir here and there,
Rushing crowds who hardly hear
Carols in the frosty air.

Turkey, tinsel, Christmas cards,
Revellers, a gaudy sight,
Above it all the church bells ringing
Joy across the night.

Have you once thought as you greet it
Is it still as true,
What is the message of this child,
What does Christmas mean to you?

CHRISTMAS BOXES

It's nearly Christmas and I can see
Lots of presents under the tree,
There's a parcel that says it's for me
So I'll jiggle it, wiggle it,
Give it a shake;
Careful though, it mustn't break,
Oh why can't Christmas come?

Here's another one, what a big box!
One thing's certain, this isn't socks.
It's heavy enough to be full of rocks!
As I jiggle it, wiggle it,
Give it a shake,
Careful though, it mustn't break.
Oh when will Christmas come?

This one is wrapped in paper with bows,
What's inside it no-one knows.
Could it be a computer do you suppose?
I'll jiggle it, wiggle it,
Give it a shake,
Careful though, it mustn't break.
Oh why can't Christmas come?

"Not to be opened till Christmas Day",
That's what the labels on them say
But Christmas is still a while away,
So I'll jiggle it, wiggle it,
Give it a shake,
Careful though, it mustn't break,
Oh Christmas, hurry and come!

POEMS

FOR THE SPRING TERM

THE SEASONS OF THE SEA

I like the sea in Springtime,
Chuckling on the sand,
Caressing with long fingers
The gently waking land.

I like the sea in Summer,
Warm and welcoming,
Lapping lazily around
Brown bodies as they swim.

I like the sea in Autumn,
Obeying the wind's will,
Caught and held in rockpools,
Cool and green and still.

But churning, raging, hurling,
Waves fierce grey and tall,
The wild and Winter ocean
I love the best of all.

THE CHOICE

What can you give the world Old Man Winter?

The starkness of bare trees against the grey sky,
The filigree trace of Jack Frost passing by,
A biting and stinging of wild wind and rain,
A garland of snow decking forest and plain.

What can you give the world, Young Maiden Spring?

A delicate sunbeam to bathe the brown hill,
The glorious gold of a new daffodil,
A mother's caress of the lamb at her side,
The breath of new life to this bare countryside.

And which will you take now oh Year So New?
Which of their robes will you take to clothe you?

My days are too short and my nights are too long,
The trees are too lonely without a bird's song,
The seeds are asleep and the fields cold and bare,
And so I must wake them – Spring's robe I will wear.

SPRING

Spring,
Is the fleecy white
Of a tiny lamb
Born last night.

Spring,
Is the shoot of green,
In the corner of the garden,
Barely seen.

Spring,
Is a lonely bird,
In the early dawn,
Softly heard.

Spring,
Is a sharp breeze,
A pale sunshine
Through the trees.

Spring,
Is a beginning.
Spring.

NEWS

"Dear me!" said the brown bulb buried so deep,
"Something has woken me up from my sleep!"
"Oh", said the little seed raising her head,
"Who is that knocking on my earthy bed?".
"What's this?" said the squirrel, "Did someone say
That there's something strange in the air today?
"I know what it is", sang a passing bird,
"Why, haven't you heard, haven't you heard?"
Then, "Come", sang the West Wind,
                          "Come out and play,
For Spring has returned to the wood today".

PANCAKE DAY

It's pancake day!
It's pancake day!
If you want pancakes, this is the way.
Take the flour and egg and milk,
Make the batter as smooth as silk,
Let the buttery pan get piping hot,
Pour in the batter – not a lot.
Let it bubble then toss it high,
Catch it quick! Don't let it fly!
Sprinkle with sugar white and sweet,
Roll it, squeeze lemon – then just eat. MMMM
It's pancake day!
It's pancake day!
I've made some delicious pancakes today.
Would you like one?

TOSSING THE PANCAKE

Have you tried to toss a pancake
Right into the air?
My Mum did once – a big mistake,
It landed in her hair.
She shook it off and down it plopped
Across the startled cat,
Who flicked it up and then it dropped
Upon the kitchen mat.
My brother with his great big feet
Kicked it to the side
Where with a movement swift and neat
The dog's mouth opened wide.
He licked his lips and gave a wink,
Mum asked: "Where did it go?
Better toss another do you think?"
And we all answered – "NO!"

THE SAD LITTLE RAIN CLOUD

There once was a sad little rain cloud,
Who gloomily sat in the sky,
"I know that everyone hates me",
He said as he drifted by.
"For they don't like showers of rain,
They'd rather have sun or snow,
For all I do is spoil their fun
They always wish that I'd go."
Then just as his raindrops were falling,
A bright sunbeam shone in the sky,
She waved at the little rain cloud
And the people laughed and said "Why!
What a beautiful coloured rainbow,
We haven't seen one for a while."
And the little rain cloud said, "Thank you,
Now I know how to make people smile."

BUTTERFLY

A sunless day,
A cold, grey sky,
Then suddenly upon the breeze,
A butterfly;
Your wings so beautiful,
So frail,
The chrysalis still shining
On your tail.
Never still,
Resting for but a moment
Where you will.
I tried to grasp you with my hand
To stick you with a pin
As foolish people do,
But with a grin
That lit your eyes of blue
Away you flew
As you had come.
But for a second
You had brushed my cheek
And I had felt the sun.

ST DAVID'S DAY

March winds,
Behind the racing clouds
One glistening shaft of sun,
Still pale, uncertain yet
That Spring might have begun.

March magic,
Now brings back the flowers.
Where dull and brown the earth,
The daffodils' warm gold
Heralds a bright rebirth.

March the first,
A day for Wales to smile,
When pride and joy abound
And hiraeth echoes still
The rugged hills around.

March music,
Joyous as daffodils
And bright as Spring sunshine;
Songs, in the lilting voice
Of language old as time.

HOW DO YOU EAT YOUR EASTER EGG?

How do you eat your Easter egg?
Do you tear the box and wrapping
And gobble it all up in one go
Before anyone sees what's happening?
DELICIOUS!

How do you eat your Easter egg?
Do you unwrap with care
Then break it into little bits
And hand some out to share?
GENEROUS!

How do you eat your Easter egg?
Do you put it away for later,
Then find that somebody's made a hole
Right through the silver paper?
SUSPICIOUS!

How do you eat your Easter egg?
Whatever you choose to do
I love the creamy, chocolaty taste
And I'm sure that you do too.
SCRUMPTIOUS!

MY EASTER BONNET

I'm going to make my Easter bonnet
Out of Mum's hat made of straw
I'm going to cover it with net,
And flowers by the score.
I think I'll have some fluffy chicks
Clustered round their mother
And the cutest rabbit on this side
And some egg shells on the other.
I'll crown it with a rainbow,
And there must be a baby lamb,
I'm going to win the prize for this
I'm very sure I am.
There, it's done I'll put in on,
It's quite a tricky manoeuvre.
Oh dear, my hat is really great –
But I have fallen over!

EASTER

When I see an Easter lily
Unblemished in purity,
I think of the perfect heart of Christ,
That broke at Gethsemene.

When I see a Springtime primrose
With its fragile simplicity,
I think of His gentle body,
That was broken at Calvary.

When I see a fragrant violet
Keep its loveliness in the gloom,
I think of the fragrant ointment,
That covered my Lord in the tomb.

When I see a Summer rosebud,
About to burst forth and be free,
I think of the resurrection
That gave freedom to you and to me.

And so I am grateful to God
For the glory of His world's bouquet
That remind me of a life
Given that mine might be saved.

POEMS

FOR THE SUMMER TERM

GOING BY BOAT

Tired of all the fog and rain
And the houses all the same,
Longing for the sun again,
We set off for sunny Spain –
This time we went by boat.

Far from land we sailed away,
Then the sky turned angry grey,
Soon we felt her lurch and sway,
Seeming though we'd never stay
For very long afloat!

Dad turned green at sight of food,
Firmly on the deck I stood,
Poor Mum didn't feel too good,
And my sister said we should
Have gone by aeroplane.

After quite a sleepless night,
Came the coast and harbour light,
Wasn't that a welcome sight!
Somehow I don't think we might
Be going by boat again!

HOLIDAYS

I love to go splash through the puddles of rain,
I love to pretend I'm driving a train,
I love to play with my motor cars small,
But I love HOLIDAYS best of all.

I love to do sums – if I get them all right,
I love to be tucked up in my bed at night,
I love to walk like a giant so tall,
But I love HOLIDAYS best of all.

For then we can ride in a speeding train,
And the sunshine has frightened away all the rain,
I carry my spade and my red rubber ball,
I do love HOLIDAYS best of all.

The sea is so tingly, I love getting wet,
And I once caught a crab in my fishing net!
And I never get tired – well, hardly at all.
Don't you love HOLIDAYS best of all?

SUMMER THOUGHTS

The golden days of Summer
Are lovelier than anything I know,
Even Autumn bonfires
Or crunching through the Christmas snow.
The evenings have the strangest magic,
Bathed in a hazy, rosy glow,
The air wafts in a balmy peace
And the sea is warm and slow.
The mornings have the freshness
Of new mown hay awash with dew,
The afternoons are lazy beneath
Clear skies of deepest blue.
The myriad gaudy petalled flowers
Welcome bees a-bumbling through.
How I wish that I could lie in Summer's sun,
With nothing else to do.

THE FUN TREE

There's a tree that stands by the old wood's edge,
Beyond Miller's stream and the hawthorne hedge,
Its old limbs are strong and knarled and brown,
While its stout trunk is scarred and overgrown.

In Winter it stands like an ugly witch,
Against the grey sky as black as pitch.
Once in its spell we are imprisoned men,
Trapped by its fingers and all doomed again.

In Summer it's thick with its leaves once more,
And rustles like leaves that break on the shore
As we steer a course to strange islands far,
Where lions and tigers and jackals are.

Pirates and robbers hide in our fun tree,
Spies who are trying to leave the country,
We keep them quite safe in our secret lair
And nobody ever knows we are there.

SUMMER'S HERE

Summer's here again,
Flowers are everywhere,
Dodging showers of rain,
Basking in the air.

Summer's here again,
Sun is warm and bright,
Stirring field and lane,
Bathing trees in light.

Summer's here again,
Bees a-buzzing home
Fat with pollen grain,
For each honeycomb.

Summer's here again,
Holidays are planned,
Packing picnic treats,
Digging in the sand.

Summer's here again,
Smokey barbeques,
Sausages or chicken,
Don't know which I'll choose!

Summer's here again,
Strawberries and cream.
Sunny days it's plain
Are a Summer dream.

HORRID!

Summer's alright as long as it's fine,
But if the sun refuses to shine,
It's horrid.

Summer's alright as long as there's sun,
But if the rain spoils all the fun,
It's horrid.

Summer's alright as long as there's sand,
But if a visit to Auntie's is planned,
It's horrid.

Summer's alright as long as there's sea,
But it's those big crabs that frighten me,
They're horrid.

Summer's alright as long as there's friends,
But if a day all alone I spend,
I'm horrid.

Summer's alright as long as it lasts,
But when the holidays all are past
It's horrid.

MERMAID'S SONG

To walk and talk
On the tall cliffs of chalk,
Is certain some people to please,
But in caves 'neath the waves
Where the angel fish plays
Lives this shimmering maid of the seas.

To rollick and frolic
In suds of carbolic
Is quite sure to have pleasures I own,
But I laze all my days
Where the sea's azure haze
Meets the sparkling white crests of the foam.

And to run in the sun
Can be ever such fun,
But I laugh in the wind and the gale;
And I whirl and I swirl
In my watery world
With the light of the moon on my tail.

A swift ride with the tide
On a ship's sturdy side
Is a fine way to spend a man's day,
But I dash and flash
Where small wavelets splash
On the red coral reefs far away.

More precious than dresses
My long silken tresses
Rich, golden as ripening corn,
And I sit where the air
Blows in gusts through my hair
In the soft crimson light of the dawn.

WHEN THE HOLIDAY COMES

When the holiday comes
I'm going to go
Down to the tumbling sea.
The sun will shine,
(It will you know)
And on the beach
Will be me!
When the holiday comes I'll dig in the sand
Down by the sparkling waves.
I'll build a castle
So fine and grand
Near the rocks and caves,
And then when the sea it comes
And tries to break it all
Down where the waves roll on,
It'll stand quite firm,
It won't ever fall,
Well, not till the holiday's gone!

SUMMER FAIR

We're having a Summer Fair,
The tables are out in the yard,
We're selling cakes and sweets
And books and birthday cards,
The toy stall is just loaded,
I brought in some stuff,
I'd like to buy some others
But Mum says I've enough.
You can throw wet sponges
At the Class Three teacher,
You get six for fifty p
So can't see how you'll miss her!
There's a treasure hunt there
And here's a counting game
And lots of raffle prizes
And guess the Teddy's name.
Over there's the bran tub
You must dig down really deep,
Last time I had some pencils
And a little bag of sweets.
Some of the mums have made bookmarks
And there's pens and pencils too
You can buy loads of presents
For only a pound or two.
That sky is getting darker,
I'll just go round again,
Oh no, I felt a splatter,
It has – it's started to rain!

OUTSIDE THIS WINDOW

Outside this window the sky is clear and blue,
Blue as silk
Wide as the ocean,
Why am I here with these sums to do?

Outside this window the grass is so green
Green and springy,
Smelling fresh,
And this is the most boring maths ever seen.

Outside this window there are hills to climb,
Hills to roll down
To follow streams,
I'm sorry, I can't make this poem rhyme.

Outside this window the sun is so bright,
Bright with the light
Of a Summer afternoon,
Oh, I'll never get these answers right.

Outside this window is playground and park,
The park with the swings
And a pond with the ducks,
I just know I'm going to get a bad mark.

Outside this window are delights I know well,
Running and laughing
Playing with friends –
Thank goodness for that there's the bell!

GROWING TOMATOES

In our greenhouse we're growing tomatoes,
I planted the seeds myself,
We've got five pots in a row
All along the shelf.

They put up some little shoots
And then came the leaves
Up through the dark brown soil,
They gently weaved.

Next came some yellow flowers,
Turning to the sun,
I watered and I fed them
Every one.

Soon there were baby tomatoes,
Small and pale and green,
I told them they were the best
I'd ever seen.

I think that made them blush,
Because they soon turned red
I picked them and I ate them
In some bread.

They were just delicious,
I'll give the next to you
So you can taste the lovely
Tomatoes I grew.

SCHOOL TRIP

Please Miss, please Miss,
I'm ready for the trip -you see
I've got cheese sandwiches
And a fizzy drink with me.
And two bags of sucky sweets
That I can share around
And a big banana
That my mother found.

Alright children,
Let's be really good today
Stand still while I count you,
Then we'll be on our way.

Please Miss, please Miss,
Can we have our snack?
Me and Jane and Miranda
Are sitting at the back.
We won't eat it all miss,
But my tummy's empty
And I've got a big bag Miss
So really there is plenty.

You can't be hungry yet,
It's only half past eight,
We're going to have a stop so
I think you ought to wait.

Continued overleaf...

Please Miss, please Miss,
We're sharing out the food,
Miranda's raspberry buns
Are very, very good.
Please Miss, please Miss,
Could the bus stop – quick,
I'm feeling a bit funny
I think I might be sick!

POEMS

TO ENJOY

EDIBLE EQUIPMENT

Sophie's fluffy banana
Is to put her pencils in,
And Megan's pink pineapple
Is a sort of backpack thing.
Josie's got a rubber
That looks just like a melon
And Emma writes with a pen
That smells just like a lemon.
Fiona's bar of chocolate
Hides a calculator,
And Janie's shiny apple
Is a pad of writing paper.
I'd better check my biscuits,
Could they be something else?
I wouldn't like to eat
A jammy dodger desk!

THAT'S NOT FAIR

Jennifer's saved her Easter egg,
And she's going to eat it today.
That's not fair!

Chloe has her birthday in the Summer
And they go outside to play.
That's not fair!

Robert's going to go ski-ing
With his favourite cousin.
That's not fair!

Adam knew in maths that twelve
Is the same as a dozen.
That's not fair!

What? You want to share
Your packet of sweets with me?
Oh now, that's fair!

SOMEBODY ELSE

I think I'll be somebody else today,
I won't be me at all.
I'll be....I'll be..... now let me see,
A wild animal stalker!
No, I'll be a tightrope walker
And practise on the garden wall.

I'm going to be something exciting today,
You won't know who I am.
I'll be....I'll be.... A shark in the sea,
With fins and tail that swishes
To frighten the little fishes,
And then I'll catch them if I can.

I think I'll live somewhere else today,
Far, far away I'll roam.
I'll go....I'll go.... To Mexico
With sombreros for the heat
And tacos and chilli to eat –
But I think I'll be glad to come home!

MAGIC SPELL

Where magic is, where fairies weave their spell,
What wondrous things will happen, who can tell?

And so to make this charm work now we must
Add several dewdrops and some twinkling dust.

And then before the magic's fully done
We'll stir it with the rays of evening sun.

Now sprinkle on fragments of your favourite dreams
The spell is almost ready now it seems.

The charm's wound up, now spirits of the night
With silver moonbeams fill the room with light

That we may see how goodness conquers all –
Cinderella, you shall go to the ball!

SATURDAYS

I love Saturdays,
They're the best day as a rule,
Because I don't get up early,
And I don't go to school.

I can lie in my bed,
And the alarm doesn't ring,
I can play with my friends,
I can do anything.

Saturdays are good days,
And in the sunshine
I just feel so happy,
Because the day is mine.

STAND AND DELIVER

Stand and deliver! I'm a highwayman,
Riding on my horse as swiftly as I can,
To shout to passengers and the coachman,
"Your money or your life please, if you can",
Because I'm ever so polite, but still a highwayman.

Stand and deliver! My name's Dirty Dick,
So you'd better hand your money over pretty quick,
'Cos at using a pistol I'm very, very slick,
Yes I know this looks just like a bit of stick,
But I'm practising today at being Dirty Dick.

Stand and deliver! I'm the traveller's enemy.
My reputation is as fiercesome as can be,
But you're lucky today, I'm going to set you free,
Because it's half past five and it's time for my tea.
But you won't forget the day you met me!

DON'T BLAME ME

Can you be blamed for something
That you really haven't done?
I don't think that would be fair,
To punish an innocent one.
Can you be given detention
When you haven't done it at all?
Can you be made to sit alone
Writing lines in the hall?
Oh good, the answer's no,
So aren't I the lucky one,
Because you see dear teacher,
It's my homework I haven't done!

SURFING

The sea's a battleground wild and strong,
To challenge a surfer as he hurtles along.
The wind whips up and whistles loud,
But on his board the surfer stands proud.
He'll struggle with all his might to gain
Mastery of the turbulent main.
The waves are walls that rear up high,
Towering over him as he flies.
The foamy crests will churn and boil
But the surfer's skill they will not foil
As he stands aloft on the rolling tide
On the mighty ocean deep and wide,
The board beneath him skimming fast
Till he reaches the safety of shore at last.
He has stayed the course, the challenge done
And such is the satisfaction won
Of knowing that once again just he
Has conquered the strength of the mighty sea.

RAILWAY VERGES

Railway verges are decorated
With a surprising array of things,
There are ubiquitous plastic bags
And inevitable bottles and tins.
There's the odd discarded jumper of course,
And one lonely shoe,
A box, a plastic chair,
And a length of piping or two.
There's earth and stones and posts and wires
And places where boys
Have been lighting fires;
A red balloon in the clutches of a tree,
A burnt out car,
A rubber tyre,
A heap of shells from a distant sea.
Then there are clumps of glossy berries,
On clambering branches.
A quivering rabbit's
Swift, inquisitive glances.
Daisies and poppies in scarlet and white
An elegant magpie
Just paused in its flight,
A glimpse of a fox's bushy tail.
What a kaleidoscope
By the side of the rail!

A FIERCE PIRATE CREW

We are a fierce pirate crew, with cutlasses in hand,
Known throughout the Seven Seas as a bold,
bloodthirsty band;
From the shores of Timbuctoo to the east of
Samarkand,
Our death defying deeds are known on sea or on the
land.

Our galleon named the Dirty Dick is sturdy stout and
strong,
With great black sails a-billowing wide as we sail
along,
She dips and heaves and plunges tall grey foaming
waves among
And as the evening darkens we speed her with a song,

Singing: "Heave away me hearties, our daily
plundering's done,
Heave away me hearties here's a fine old bottle of
rum!"
We'll sit and tell bold tales until we see the morning
sun
Then look out all you jolly tars, for here the pirates
come!

With the cry of "Pirate galley!" the bravest Captain's
eyes
Are filled with greatest horror as the Dirty Dick he
spies,
For soon along the quivering plank his gallant crew all
dies.
Treachery is on the sea when the Jolly Roger flies.

MR WOFFLE

At the bottom of our garden,
Where no-one ever goes,
There's the strangest little creature
With pink and turned up nose.

I can call him Mr Woffle,
Since we've become good friends
And often call at his small house,
Just where the garden ends.

He isn't very tall you know,
About six inches high.
He says, "Good morning", when I pass
And winks his little eye.

He wears a coat of cabbage leaves,
A radish for a hat,
Trimmed with a plume of carrot ferns,
And shoes of berries black.

I'm the only one who sees him,
Because he's very shy.
We are the very best of friends
Mr Woffle and I.

STEPS IN TIME

I like to hear of long ago,
When little girls like me,
Wore dresses made of silk and lace,
And sat still as can be.

They would spend simply hours and hours
Just curling up their hair,
Or balancing books on their heads
With noses in the air.

Their boots were soft and buttoned up,
Their pantaloons were long,
They spent their afternoons engaged
In needlework or song.

They never spoke till spoken to,
They always were so good.
Imagine me so ladylike
No – I don't think that you could!

POEMS

ABOUT CREATURES

THE BAD TEMPERED BEE

A bad tempered bee was buzzing
Around the garden flowers,
He buzzed and buzzed
In a bad tempered fuzz
For hours and hours and hours.

"I don't want to look for pollen,
And I don't want to fly all day,
I find that a rose
Tickles my nose
All I want to do is play."

His mother got crosser and crosser,
She said: "Now listen to me,
In the hive you will stay,
With no honey today
For that's only for good little bees."

MR SQUIRREL

Who is that rustling through the dead leaves?
Who is that scampering across the bare trees?
Who is that whisking his tail in the sun?
Who is that gathering his nuts one by one?
Who is that nestling in his hole so small
And curling up tightly into a ball?
Perhaps you can guess, but let's go and peep.
Why, it's Mr Squirrel – and he's fast asleep!

DINOSAURS AND DODOS

The dinosaurs and dodos
Were once quite free to roam
Through forests and through jungles
That they could call their home.

The dinosaurs soon vanished
Millions of years ago,
No-one is really certain,
Why or even how.

Then the lonely dodos
Eventually found
That there were not so many
Big forests spreading round.

Man came with all his power
To roam the land instead
And now the dinosaurs and dodos
Were both completely dead.

Continued overleaf...

And as the forests dwindled,
The animals dwindled too,
Gorillas, pandas, lions,
Were only seen in zoos.

And as a boy peered at them
Behind their prison bars,
He asked where they had come from,
Were they, like him, from Mars?

Oh no, his father told him,
On earth these creatures passed
Through forests full of leafy trees.
"What is a tree?" he asked.

THE GOLDEN GROWLER

The Golden Growler came in a box,
A very pleasant
Birthday present,
Much better than hankies or socks.

The Golden Growler's a lion,
Who sits and sleeps
And never keeps
What he's meant to keep an eye on.

The Growler's fur is golden
But head on paws,
He never roars,
To show the world he's a bold one.

The Golden Growler guards my treasure,
But no sound slips
Through whiskered lips,
Set in a wide smile of pleasure.

The Golden Growler's not tall,
But he's my friend
So I pretend
He's the bravest lion of all.

SLOW

Slow the tortoise creeping by
Watching with a flickering eye,
Wondering if he'll ever reach
That far green and tasty leaf.

Like a map in rough relief,
Onward moves this lettuce thief,
Pushing through the leaves and grass,
Ants and beetles watch him pass.

Still he goes with measured tread,
Determined thrust of wrinkled head,
Across the lawn, along the path,
With the prize in sight at last.

Now he's there, with blissful munch
Indulging in his favourite lunch;
Just five metres he has gone,
But for Slow a marathon!

THE ANTIQUE ELEPHANT

Right at the back of a dusty old shop,
In the dingiest, dirtiest corner you've seen,
(If by some chance you should happen to stop)
There's a tiny black elephant standing between
The stuffy remains of a glassy-eyed bird
And a large and lopsided Victorian vase.
Of his days before these not a person has heard,
But once I had seen him I just couldn't pass,
Wondering if ever he felt rather sad
Because he was here with a price on his 'nose'.
Or whether he secretly felt rather glad
Of a rest from adventures on strange foreign shores.
Were you once garlanded, trimmed and bedecked
In rich Eastern purple or gold of Cathey,
To parade at the festival of some ancient sect,
Mid prayers and sweet incense on some gorgeous day?
Oh what could he tell, carved creature of ebony,
Eyes of black jet and tusks of white ivory,
And yet he remains there, quite quite undeterred
By the lopsided vase and the stuffy old bird.

MOPSY AND ME

I have a rabbit all furry and brown,
I decided to call her Mopsy;
Her coat is long and as soft as down,
And her ears are warm and floppy.

Her eyes are bright, shiny and beady,
Her whiskers are straight and silver,
She's round and fat and ever so greedy
And her nose is always a-quiver.

My Dad has made her a beautiful hutch
In the garden beneath the Beech tree,
She never seems to do very much,
Just shuffles and looks at me.

Sometimes I think she is seeming to say
"I am happy from dawn to day's end
With such a nice place to rest or play
And you as my very best friend."

NINE LIVES

A cat has got nine lives they say,
And I think that must be true,
For when he was small,
Ours fell off a wall
And down a well – and lost two!

He only had seven lives left then,
And he got in a terrible fix,
He was trapped in a hole
That was once meant for coal,
And so that left him just six.

Before long he soon lost another
As he climbed through the dishwasher door,
We pulled on his tail his tail
And heard his loud wail
As he dripped all over the floor.

With only five lives left he wandered
Over the garden wall,
Then got stuck up a tree
And couldn't get free
And the firemen had to be called.

I hope he hangs on to the next four,
And loses his adventurous desire
For I love my old cat
And I've told him that
So I hope he'll just sleep by the fire.

THE GERBIL'S ESCAPE

Today the gerbil's got out of his cage,
I think the bars were bitten
And now he's got himself downstairs
And is completely hidden.
Oh, there he goes, I saw his tail,
Underneath the armchair,
Move it quickly so he's cornered,
Too late, he's over there.
Now he's rustling in the bookcase
I can hear his scratchy feet
Try to tempt him out with something,
That gerbils like to eat.
Now he's heading for the telly,
Do gerbils like to view?!
He'll be in trouble if that cable
He decides to chew.
Look out, he's just emerging,
Catch him please somehow
I can hear the catflap moving
He could be eaten now!
Phew, you've done it, thank you,
What an escapade,
Come on gerbil you are going
Back inside your cage.

WALKIES - FOR CHARLIE

There's a magic word in our house
And it causes much delight,
With tail a-wagging, nose a-nuzzling
And eyes that sparkle bright.
"Walkies".

When we go to fetch the collar
And rattle the long lead,
She bounds along, she runs around,
"Is it now?" she pleads
Walkies.

As soon as I put my coat on
And tuck my hands in gloves
She knows that now the time has come,
The time she really loves,
Walkies.

I couldn't be more popular
If I was a millionaire,
And I am glad and she is glad
To be out in the crisp fresh air.
Walkies.

FAIRGROUND FISH

Darts to throw,
Twenty one,
A golden fish
I have won,
Into a bag
Not very big,
Get him home,
Quick as quick.
Buy a bowl,
A bit of weed,
A little box
Of special feed.
Add the water,
Not too cold,
Then a lovely
Flash of gold,
Flick of tail
Quiver of fin,
Open the bag,
Pour him in.
There he goes
Swirl and swish,
Happy now,
My golden fish.

PUDGIE THE BUDGIE

We've got to look after our neighbours' budgie,
Pudgie.
While they will be away
We've offered to have our neighbours' budgie,
Pudgie,
Just for a couple of days.
They say he's an easy to care for budgie,
Pudgie,
Let us hope that's true,
Now then,who's a very pretty budgie,
Pudgie?
I'm talking to you.
He's not a performer our neighbours' budgie
Pudgie
Sometimes he might sing
But most of the time our neighbours' budgie
Pudgie,
Doesn't do a thing.
He lives up to his name our neighbours' budgie
Pudgie,
And simply sits and eats,
Not much noise from our neighbours' budgie,
Pudgie.
Just an occasional tweet.
They're back tomorrow so the neighbours' budgie
Pudgie
Will get a present from Spain
Which I hope will cheer up our neighbours' budgie,
Pudgie.
I can't wait till they go again.

POEMS

ABOUT THE WEATHER

WIND

The wind blows softly through the grasses,
Making them ripple as it passes.

The wind blows strongly through the trees,
Shaking and rustling the trembling leaves.

The wind whips up the wintry waves,
Tossing them over the rocks and caves.

The storm winds lash the rain swept town,
Raging and hurling up and down.

The sun comes out and dries the rain,
The wind dies down and is quiet again.

WINTER WIND

Gathering over the far horizon
It curls its long cumulus tail,
And building, barging, battling,
Blowing,
It spews out its rattling hail.
It chivvies and charges
And churns up the seas,
It whistles down streets
And it whirls round the trees.
It rattles the windows
It bangs the back gate,
A gale is expected
Could be storm force eight.
The weatherman's warnings are heeded,
But wait –
Turning to face the far horizon
The winter wind wriggles away,
It's frosty, it's crisp
And the cold sun is rising,
But the Winter wind's gone
For today.

RAIN – AGAIN!

Rain, rain, rain, rain, rain, rain,
Surely it can't be raining again?
For yesterday it rained all day
It looks like it's the same today.
Rain, rain, rain, rain, rain, rain.
I can't believe it's raining again.

Rain, rain, rain, rain, rain, rain.
Yes I thought so, raining again.
From where, oh where, does it all come down,
Beating and bouncing on the ground?
Rain, rain, rain, rain, rain, rain,
You see, I told you, it's raining again.

Rain, rain, rain, rain, rain, rain.
Here comes another shower again.
Put on your boots, your mackintosh,
And out you go with a splish and splosh.
Rain, rain, rain, plip, plip, plop.
What? Well I never! It has – it's stopped!

RAINSTORM

Sleeting and sheeting
The rainstorm comes,
Beating on roofs
Like an army's drums,
Stutter and splutter
The wind in the trees
Scatters the drops
With moaning wheeze.
Gushing and rushing
The gutter's a stream,
The pavements reflect
The lamp light's gleam.
Hurrying and scurrying
Crowds go by
Under the heavy
And leaden sky.
Sniffling and snuffling
Home they go,
To warm their bones
And dry their toes.

I LIKE THE RAIN

I think I like the rain you know,
I like the way the pavements glow,
And you can see the traffic light
Upside down and winking bright.
I like the way the clouds roll by
Like grey maned horses up on high.
I like the sound on roof and pane
A surging, waning soft refrain.
I like the glistening garden's face,
That rain has washed in every place.
I like the smell of dampened grass
After the storm of rain has passed.
Yes, I do, I like the rain.
I hope we have a shower again.

LOOK IT'S SNOWING

"Look it's snowing!" the children cried,
And suddenly books were ignored
And eyes were turned to the feathery sky
And the flakes that covered the yard.
No Maths or English could take the place
Of the transformation there
As the trees grew delicate gloves
Over their branches bare,
And the walls grew an extra layer
And the slide a soft white hat,
Now lessons were second rate
As they watched a neighbouring cat,
Carefully leave his paw prints
Like writing on a sheet
And pens were abandoned in hopes
Of a special snowy treat.
At last the teacher granted
The wish that none dare say,
"Look, it's snowing children",
We'll finish lessons for today."

ON A SNOWY DAY

On a snowy day I like to watch
As the flakes tumble slowly down,
Covering roof and hedges and lawns
Transforming all the town.
On a snowy day when the air is still
And the sky is grey and dark,
I wrap up warm in scarf and boots
And take a walk in the park.
I look for a sheet that's white and clear
And then I boldly go
Making my footprints like a giant
Deep in the untouched snow.
I like to pretend there's no-one else,
I'm exploring a brand new place
As the snowflakes fall onto my sleeve
As delicate as woven lace.
And then I turn and head for home
With my cheeks and my nose aglow
And close the door and sit by the fire
And watch the darkening snow.

THE SUN SPEAKS

The sun on the sea
Is calling to me,
It's saying:
"Come out and swim.
My water is blue
And waiting for you
So why don't you plunge in?"

The sun on the sand
Calls over the land,
It's saying:
"Come out and play
You can dig, you can run,
It will be such fun
So come and enjoy today".

The sun on the hill
Is shining still
And saying:
"Come out and walk.
Forget all your care
In the warm Summer air,
Lie on the grass and talk."

The sun's going down,
Across the whole town,
And saying:
"I'm having a nap,
But just keep your eyes on
The Eastern horizon,
Tomorrow I'll be back!"

I LOVE IT

The holidays have just begun,
And I am lying in the sun,
They call and call but I won't come,
I love it.

The sun is hot and shines on me,
With suncream I am covered – see,
I hear the drone of bumble bee,
I love it.

The rose's scent wafts gently by,
I see a gold winged butterfly,
I turn my head and close my eyes,
I love it.

Here there's only me and sun,
No boring school work to be done,
My thoughts and I are simply one,
I love it.

Across the lawn the shadows creep,
Mum comes out and takes a peep,
But I have fallen fast asleep.
She loves it!

RAINBOW

Red is the colour of a warming Summer dawn,
Orange lights the marigolds nodding round the lawn,
Yellow paints the sand dunes on a sunny day,
Green are the hills where we roll and play.
Blue is the sky without a cloud in sight,
Indigo tints the clouds on a stormy night.
Violet is the pansy's face in the rockery,
The rainbow paints a picture that we all can see.

STORM

Heavy air,
Phew it's warm,
Think we'll get
A thunderstorm,
Sky grows black,
Inky clouds,
Distant rumblings
Getting loud.
There's a flash,
Now it comes,
Thunder beats
On Heaven's drums,
And another,
Forked and bright,
Clap so loud,
What a fright!
Windows rattle
Dog is scared,
Here's another,
Be prepared!
Easing off now,
Spots of rain,
Hope that storm
Won't come again.

THE QUEEN OF ICE

I am the Queen of Ice
And oh,
In a trice,
I'll show
How special I can be,
Now watch the Queen of Ice
With frosty call
Entice
To fall,
Each leaf from Summer tree.
I am the Queen of Ice,
I'll go
With feet
Of snow
And sleet
To freeze the lake and pond.
I am the Queen of Ice
My fingers hold
In vice
So cold
All here and all beyond.
I am the Queen of Ice,
My bold
Device
To hold
The earth within my spell,
So heed the Queen of Ice,
This chill,
My price,
My will
To rule the Winter well.

Printed in April 2023
by Rotomail Italia S.p.A., Vignate (MI) - Italy